AF564510

CREATING YOUR FUTURE

CREATING YOUR FUTURE

SHALINI RAJNEESH
IAS

and

USHA VASU

Foreword by

JUSTICE SHIVARAJ V. PATIL
Former Judge
Supreme Court of India

DEEP & DEEP PUBLICATIONS PVT. LTD.
F-159, Rajouri Garden, New Delhi-110027

CREATING YOUR FUTURE

ISBN 978-81-8450-381-4

Typeset by S.S. COMPOSERS
3190, Mohindra Park, Shakur Basti, Delhi-110034.

Printed in India at MAYUR ENTERPRISES
WZ Plot No. 3, Gujjar Market, Tihar Village, New Delhi-110018.

Published by DEEP & DEEP PUBLICATIONS PVT. LTD.
F-159, Rajouri Garden, New Delhi-110027.
Phones: 25435369, 25440916
E-mail: ddpbooks@yahoo.co.in • ddpubs@gmail.com
Showroom:
2/13, Ansari Road, Daryaganj, New Delhi-110002 • Telefax: 23245122

This book is dedicated to

My daughter
Muskan
Dr. Shalini Rajneesh

My younger son
Arun Vasudeva Rao
Usha Vasu

Contents

EXERCISE 5

UNDERSTANDING OUR TENDENCIES AND THE FIRST 'C'

EXERCISE 6

INTERNAL DEVELOPMENT

EXERCISE 7

ANALYZE YOUR FEARS

EXERCISE 8

LIMITLESS THINKING

EXERCISE 9

AFFIRMATIONS AT THE BEGINNING OF THE DAY

Justice Shivaraj V. Patil

Former Judge
Supreme Court of India

Foreword

I am delighted to deliver this foreword to the book titled "CREATING YOUR FUTURE". I read the contents of the book with keenness and interest am duly and deeply impressed by the contents of the book having regard to the purpose sought to be achieved, the quality and utility and the way they are presented, integrating various aspects to achieve the intended object. I have every good reason to think that the appeal an impact of the book will be significant particularly on the young minds, who are interested and wiling to know as to how to create their future to be somebody to be necked with.

Articles written by Dr. Shalini Rajneesh I.A.S. were published in Kannada News Paper 'Vijay Karnataka'. They are compiled and being published by Gulbarga University in the form of a book under the title 'Nimma Bhavishya Nimma Kayyalli'. The English translation of the same titled as 'Creating Your Future' is being brought out to reach larger section of society usefully and rightly so in my opinion.

Our country has vast human resources. I am clear and confident that it is only the Youngisthan that can make a better Hindustan, in the present scenario obtaining in the Country. 253 million women and 268 million men together 521 million between the age group of 12 and 35 constitute the strength and spirit of India with the added power of voting given to them at 18. May be this is the reason why ageing leaders have suddenly woken up and try to woo young voters. It is strange that as of now 97% of youth have no access to the internet, 41% are not able to watch television 67.9% are unaware of the internet, 86.9% do not go to movie theatres, 76.3% never listen to radio, 4.1% read English newspapers and 25% are studying while 7.8% work as agricultural laborers and 74% are engaged in jobs other than farming. But the large majority of them are caught in the cycle of poverty. These are the few figures given by Sri Suresh Nimbalkar of Hansa Research compiled in 2008.

In this age of information, advanced science and technology and transport and communication, there seems unprecedented mobilization among young people and they have started realizing that they should not remain passive onlookers but must be active participants in all developments that take place in the country and rightly so, in my opinion. The children need attention and protection and the elderly need care and help. It is the youth who are vitally concerned with the spirit and the strength they have. The future belongs to them. They have to work to create a future of their choice and make India a better place to live in. In other words, they should strive and build rainbow India in which every one in this country should feel happy and take pride that he is born in this country. It is not wise to underestimate the abilities, potentialities, aspirations and ambitions of youth. The mindset that young people need supervision and they should proceed on the dotted lines and move in the direction drawn by the elderly and aged, needs a change. The youth are brilliant and better informed with exposure to modern developments and advancement in science and technology including information. They are abreast and up-to-date in the contemporary context and are capable of taking appropriate decisions not only in the matter of choosing their careers but also causes as citizens. May be, at times youth need guidance that the aged can give with their experience. We require both the strength of youth the maturity of the old. In other words, matured heads should rest on the young shoulders. "Invasion of Armies can be resisted but not an idea whose time has come"—Victor Hugo. In my view such time has come and the youth can bring the desired change for the good of the people of this country. Youth as they are in large numbers, have a tremendous role to play and a huge opportunity is there to build economy and to change the destiny of millions of less fortunate, unfortunate, the sick, the suffering, the disadvantaged, neglected, excluded and all vulnerable sections of people in the Country. Youth may bring welcome change by silent revolution through ballot realizing that the vote is a powerful and useful tool to do so. Look at history, the youth made fundamental difference in the thinking and working of the people, recent instances being of Rajiv Gandhi and Barack Obama. We have shining Youth achievers in all fields. May be they are not in lime light or do not get the publicity they deserved.

This book is result of reflects too, the hard work, commitment, experience, knowledge and the collaborative efforts of both the Authors—Dr. Shalini Rajneesh and Smt. Usha Vasu. The academic, practical and administrative experience with men and matter in the public field of Dr. Shalini Rajneesh and Smt. Usha Vasu's contribution with her knowledge, and varied experience in conducting workshops on the subject "creating future" for over a decade have certainly enhanced the intrinsic value of the book. Thus, the book, is a combination of the knowledge embedded in the science of psychology, sociology and management. They deserve both appreciation and congratulations.

It is said and it is so "Sea is common to all, some take pearls, some take fishes and some come out with just wet legs. World is common to us, we take what we look for". Everyone has something hidden in him/her but what is required is to discover dream and develop. "A man asked sculptor how do you make such beautiful idols from stone? He said idols are already hidden there I just remove unwanted stone".

In my view, this book works as a motivator and catalyst in the direction of creating one's future. It is plain to read and simple to practice having illustrations, diagrams and statements. It helps every willing and interested youth to create his/her desired future. This book is of immense use to help the youth to make their meaningful and useful contribution in the development of the country. Sir Winston Churchill said "some find difficulty in every opportunity and others find opportunity in every difficulty." It has proper reflections in creating positive attitude, clarity, confidence and mindset in going ahead to create future for the youth. Development of individual leads to development of the country. It also helps the youth to discover what they are and what they are capable of achieving. There cannot be straight jacket formula for everyone. One has to discover his potentiality and design his ways to succeed in the set-up or circumstances he is placed. This book leads one in that direction scientifically.

I hope this book will be well received looking to its worth and utility. It is coming out at the time when such books are imperatively and urgently needed in the present times in our Country. The readers and particularly the youth will stand to gain meaningfully and usefully in creation of fruitful future for them. I wish the Authors to bring out some more books which may be constructive and meaningful in human development particularly keeping in view the good of the common man.

(JUSTICE SHIVARAJ V. PATIL)

Introduction

If you were asked to write the names of people whom you consider to be successful, how many can you list out? May be you can count them on your finger tips or make a list of a few hundred after thinking hard enough. **But in a world of billions of human beings, why is it that only a few become successful?** Do others not wish to be recognized for their distinctions? How are the ordinary people different from the extra-ordinary ones?

The study of human behaviour has always fascinated us. More than academic knowledge it is the interaction with a variety of people, which makes us comprehend this subject deeply. **No two thumb impressions are alike, leave alone the similarities among individuals.** Genetic factors coupled with environmental factors build a person. The body language, posture, ego, thoughts or actions, all vary so widely among people that, the more we try to decipher it the more complex it becomes.

Life is too precious to be wasted away in trial and error. Confronted with failure we feel that we need some direction, someone to look into our life and tell us whether we are going in the right direction and what more we need to do to make our dreams come true. **Though, we get a lot of advice from our parents, teachers, elders or peers yet our intellect does not accept it, unless we have tested it out.** The secrets unraveled in this book are meant to be tested out and adopted, if found to be worthy of it!

We try to classify people as gross, less refined, more refined, from our own perspective but everyone is right depending on his or her stage of refinement. As we are all so interdependent in our day-to-day life, we need to choose strategies for minimising other's negative influence and maximising our positive achievements. The bottom line is that a person who is better equipped to face life is the cynosure of all eyes. And who does not want to be one? **The book, 'Creating your Future', is for such people who want to be success conscious, who want to work towards internal development and for people who want to move from being nobody to somebody and from being somebody to a significant person.** A ship is quite safe in the harbour, but that is not what it is meant for! It should be well equipped to traverse its journey, safely and successfully.

This book was born after intense study. People do express that they want to become successful in life but when their efforts do not yield the desired results, they blame it on luck. **This book de-mystifies the concept of luck.** The intention of the authors is to make our youth realize their real potential to lead this life meaningfully and successfully. **This book intends to empower the reader to carve his or her destiny.** It pulls you out from desperations and fills you up with an unprecedented energy to drive your cherished agenda. The techniques explained in the book are extremely simple, logical and practical. You get a feeling that you always knew this and wonder why you did not apply it so far.

The pre-condition for reading this book is that you should have an open mind, just as a parachute has to be kept open before taking a dive! Once you start reading this book, you have to be doing the exercises on your self, then documenting them and reviewing your own outcome from time to time. We can assure you of the results, if the principles shared in this book are understood and applied whole-heartedly. Read it second time to understand, appreciate, internalize and document what you have read after doing all the exercises given. Read it the third time and if it has impacted you, then apply it in your life and also give this book as a gift to someone you care for. **A successful life is waiting for you. Walk tall with your 'aim', run with 'confidence' and fly with your 'achievements.'**

Happy transformation...

DR. SHALINI RAJNEESH
shalini.rajneesh2@gmail.com
USHA VASU
usha76vasu@gmail.com

EXERCISE

Create Your Own Future

'Do you believe that you can create your own future?' When this question is asked, most of the people will say 'no', some people will say 'yes' and some will say 'don't know'. This is mainly due to our well entrenched belief in Karma Philosophy or fatalism. Let us see what you think about this. May we request you to write down the answer that comes to your mind and then we will help you to review it at the end of this book?

We are now going to talk about how to create our future. **Every second that we spend fruitfully today, determines our future.** Therefore, the most important step is to find out as to how we are spending our day. Please take a pen and a paper. Select any active weekday. Weekday is preferred as the normal activities have to take place on that day. Week-end gives a feeling of relaxation and there is a tendency to postpone our commitments. Start classifying 24 hours of the day under the following categories.

Physical: Our sleep time, getting ready time, exercise time, walking time can be classified under this head.

Social: The time that we spend for social calls, social visits can be classified here.

Emotional: The time that we spend with our family, loved ones or any time which gives satisfaction when some work is done which is close to the heart, can be put under this head.

Intellectual: The time that we spend in serious reading, cross word puzzle, intellectual games, etc. can be classified here.

Spiritual: The time spent in prayer, meditation, discourses, etc. can be classified here.

Work/Studies: The time we spend in our work environment, including traveling to and fro to place of work can be classified here.

Mental: If we are spending any time on developing our mind, it can be classified here.

Any Other: If there are any other activities like watching TV, reading newspaper, etc. which cannot be classified in any of the above categories, can be classified here.

When you total all the time allotted under each category, you will normally notice that the time allotted towards your mental activity will be very minimal. This is an area which requires our attention, if we have to become successful in life. Most of us do not know as to what can be put under mental activity. For the time being, whatever you feel is the mental activity can be put under this head.

Please review your opinion on what you had thought as mental activity, whether actually fits into it or not, after reading this book.

CONCEPT

1

Knowing about the Mind

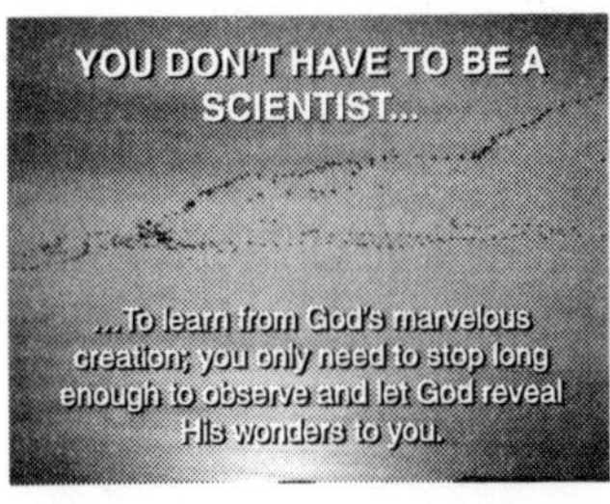

It is a well known fact that before any concrete action is taken; it has to appear in our mind first. The idea of building a house has to appear in our mind first and then it takes shape in the form of consulting an architect, to draw a plan, a civil engineer to give the estimate and a bank manager to fund the project. So, it is important to know a little about the mind. We usually think that each one of us has only one mind, which is more of an abstract term. **But it has been scientifically proved that human mind has 3 forms: conscious mind, sub-conscious mind and super-conscious mind.** The first two minds are within us, but the super-conscious mind is without. It is the mind of our extended self. Let us understand what is the relative strength of each of these forms and how can we use this knowledge to 'create our future'.

CONSCIOUS MIND POWER

Our conscious mind is the part of our mind that

thinks. That's why most people use their conscious mind power to solve problems and to achieve their goals. The conscious mind is like a Judge. It is logical. It can distinguish between good and bad, right and wrong, past, present and future. It sleeps when we sleep and works logically when we are awake.

The most important power of the conscious mind is the power to decide. It has the power to decide as to what information should enter into our sub-conscious mind, yet most of us are not exercising this power. Instead, we let rubbish enter our sub-conscious mind and thus garbage in leads to garbage out.

Our conscious mind also has the power to re-programme our sub-conscious mind, mainly through repetition. For instance, remember the first time we learnt to drive a car, when we had to consciously think of which peddle to step and which gear to shift? But now, we no longer have to consciously think of these actions. They have become automatic, i.e. we are able to do it sub-consciously. **Through repetition, we have programmemed our sub-conscious mind. Once it is in our sub-conscious, it becomes automatic.** While it's true for driving a car, it is also true for achieving success in life!

SUB-CONSCIOUS MIND POWER

The conscious mind power is limited, as compared to the sub-conscious mind power and super-conscious mind power. The sub-conscious mind is like a robot. It cannot distinguish between good and bad, right and wrong, past, present and future. It works all the 24 hours of the day. It works even when we are sleeping. It does not understand logic. It takes whatever is fed into it, like a servant, without discrimination. ***It has a huge potential as the sub-conscious mind motivates our conscious mind to take action.***

Our sub-conscious mind plays many different roles in our life. There are eight functions of the sub-conscious.

1. It works as a memory bank (like a computer).
2. It regulates involuntary functions (heart, digestion, etc.).

3. It functions as the seat of emotions.
4. It functions as the seat of imagination,
5. It controls habit.
6. It functions as a dynamo-directing energy that motivates us.
7. It is like a magnet. It has the power to attract things that resonate with its beliefs.
8. It is like radar. It sends and receives information to and from the super-conscious mind.

By using our sub-conscious mind power, we can become success-conscious.

SUPER-CONSCIOUS MIND POWER

Napoleon Hill called it the **Infinite Intelligence**. Scientists call it the **Universal Mind**. Some books or metaphysics gurus sum everything up as the **Unconscious Mind**. There is only one super-conscious mind (the **Universal Mind**), to which all of our minds are connected.

It helps us to make good decision, since it has **Infinite Intelligence**. It has all the answers we want.

It is the source of all true invention. Great inventors had mastered the technique of receiving great ideas from the super-conscious mind.

It helps us to achieve our goals. The super-conscious mind is like a mega computer that orchestrates the activities in every little computer connected to it. By impressing our goal upon our sub-conscious mind, our super-conscious mind will respond accordingly. The right people will start appearing in our life, opportunities will come and direction will be provided to strengthen our efforts, if necessary. Everything will be set in motion to help us achieve our desire. ***Once we truly understand the super-conscious mind power, we will realize that success is not just a function of luck.***

Our conscious mind is connected to our sub-conscious mind, which in turn is connected to the super-conscious mind. The conscious mind is not connected directly to the super-conscious mind. We rely on our sub-conscious mind to send and receive information to and from the super-conscious mind.

RELATIONSHIP BETWEEN CONSCIOUS, SUB-CONSCIOUS AND SUPER-CONSCIOUS MIND

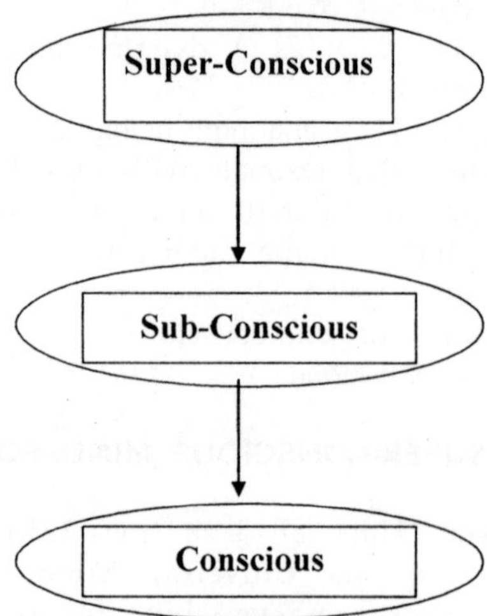

As our conscious mind impresses our desire upon our sub-conscious mind, our sub-conscious mind will impress it upon the super-conscious mind which will then conspire to make it happen, as what **Ralph Waldo Emerson said, "Once you make a decision, the universe conspires to make it happen".**

RULES OF THE MIND

It is important here to know the Rules of The Mind as professed by the late Charles Tebbets, "the grandmaster of hypnotheraphy":

(1) Every thought or idea causes a physical reaction

The mind can make you sick or keep you well. Ideas that have strong emotional content almost always reach the sub-conscious mind, because it is the feeling mind. Once accepted, these ideas continue to produce the same body reactions over and over again. In order to eliminate or change chronic negative bodily reactions we must reach the sub-conscious and change the idea responsible for that reaction.

(2) What's expected tends to be realized

The brain and the nervous system respond only to mental images, either self-induced or from the external world. The mental image formed becomes the blueprint, and the sub-conscious mind uses every means at its disposal to carry out the plan. That's why it is important to always maintain a positive state of mind because ***we become what we think about.***

(3) Imagination is more powerful than knowledge while dealing with the mind

This is an important rule to remember in controlled meditation. Any idea accompanied by a strong emotion such as anger, hatred, love, or political and religious beliefs usually cannot be modified through the use of reason. In using controlled meditation we can form images in the sub-conscious mind and can remove, alter or amend the old ideas.

(4) Opposing ideas cannot be held at one and the same time

Many people try to hold opposing ideas simultaneously. A man might believe in honesty and expect his children to be honest, and all the while be engaged daily in slightly dishonest business practices. He may try to justify this; however, he cannot escape the conflict and its effect upon his nervous system. ***This is also called the law of conflict.***

(5) Once an idea has been accepted by the sub-conscious mind, it remains until it is replaced by another idea

The longer it is held, the more it tends to become a fixed habit or thought pattern. This is how habits are formed, both good and bad.

(6) An emotionally induced symptom tends to cause organic change if persisted long enough

We are a mind in a body and the two cannot be separated. Therefore, if we continue to fear ill-health and constantly talk about it, over a period of time, organic changes are bound to occur.

(7) Each suggestion acted upon creates less opposition to successive suggestion

Minor victories lead to major victories. Small commitment leads to large commitments. An object in motion tends to stay in motion, whether it's a speeding car, an emotion, a habit, or a belief. ***This can also be called the rule of compound suggestion.***

(8) While dealing with the sub-conscious mind and its functions, the greater the conscious effort, the less the sub-conscious response

This proves why sometimes "will-power" doesn't really work! If one has insomnia we have learnt that "the harder one tries to go to sleep, the more wide awake one becomes." The thumb rule while dealing with the sub-conscious mind is, TAKE IT EASY. This means we must work to develop a positive mental expectancy that our problem can be and will be solved.

When we are born, our sub-conscious mind is crystal clear and pure. But as we grow, our sub-conscious mind takes whatever we feed into it like a sponge absorbing water, be it clean, dirty or colored. It can play havoc in our lives. Let us take the example of Guddi.

Guddi was born with other two sisters who were very beautiful. She was dark and so was treated as the black sheep of the family. Her parents, relatives, neighbors, friends and many others compared her to her beautiful sisters and branded her as dark and ugly. **She was highly intelligent, talented and hard working. But the garbage which was fed very strongly into her sub-conscious mind was that she is dark and ugly.** It was so strong that it took hold of her completely. She did not know how to handle her sub-conscious mind and failed miserably in all areas of her life as she allowed only the point of her not being good looking, sweeping away all her other excellent qualities. So it is important to handle our sub-conscious mind which can be of a great help to us in lifting us up.

The confusion we see in the minds of people is mainly due to untrained sub-conscious mind. It is unfortunate that least time is spent on understanding it and training it. It is therefore of utmost importance to train it from the childhood to create happy human beings.

CONCEPT

2

Thought Forms

We have to understand about the thought forms, which are the basis for training our sub-conscious mind. Thought forms are nothing but vibrations produced by us. **Vibrations play an important role in the universe.** The human ear has receptors that can detect sound frequencies ranging from 16 vibrations to 20,000 vibrations per second. The human ear is capable of hearing many of the sounds produced in nature, but certainly not all. Some low frequencies like a heart beat of 1 or 2 Hz (cycles per second) can not be heard, just like sonar sounds produced by dolphins which are of very high frequency. Any frequency that is below the human range is known as infrasound. It is so low that it may be detected by a creature with big ears, such as an Elephant. Ultrasound, on the other hand, is above the range of the human ear. Bats, whales, tortoises, and dolphins use ultrasound for navigation. Most bats can detect frequencies as high as 100,000 Hz!

Similarly, heat has 1,50,000 vibrations per second. It can be detected by the nerve endings of our skin. If the vibrations are more than this, it burns our skin. Likewise, light also emits vibrations. The ultraviolet light having higher vibrations, cannot be seen by us, whereas cats and owls can detect it. **It is said that our thoughts also have vibrations of very high frequency which cannot be felt by us.** It can pass through any medium like solid, liquid and gas easily! It can travel any distance. Our thought vibrations are sent out into the universe on a regular basis.

Whatever happens in our life is due to law of attraction. It is neither by accident nor by coincidence. Our thought forms attract what we want from the universe. ***This is the secret of success.*** All the successful men and women send powerful thought forms about their desire of success which gets manifested. They move from one success to another success. Let us take the example of Mahatma Gandhi. He was attracting whatever he wanted to achieve by strong affirmations and thought forms.

Our thoughts create our future. If we are careful of our thought forms and entertain only positive thoughts, we end up becoming successful. If we send negative thought forms such as ill-health, debt and failure in whatever we do, we end up getting what we ask for! If we sit back and analyze our present position, it will be a reflection of our thoughts. Happy thoughts keep us happy. Unhealthy thoughts keep us unhealthy. If one has the habit of cribbing and complaining, we can notice that we will be in a situation of cribbing and complaining all the time. We attract it through the law of Universe. **The thought that takes its birth in our mind expands and manifests in the real situation in front of our eyes**. So one should be careful about one's thought patterns.

> 'Thoughts lead to Action, Action leads to Habit, Habit leads to Character and Character leads to our Future or Destiny'.

In olden days it was a usual practice to offer a particular prayer to a particular God for a specific period of 21 days or 41 days or so. It was being followed very religiously, in anticipation of good things happening at the end. It may be seen here that a continuous message was being sent through our thought forms for desirable event to happen, both to our sub-conscious mind and the universe. After the stipulated period, most of the time, the prayer would have been answered. **Praying for good things to happen used to become a habit by virtue of repeating it for a specified period.** Our ancestors knew how to make use of our sub-conscious mind!

Let us see how to make use of thought forms in our daily life. Imagine that Lakshmi had borrowed Rs. 5000 from Gowri with a promise that she would return it by tomorrow. But today she realized that she is not in a position to return it to her by tomorrow. Normally Lakshmi would avoid calling up Gowri or answering her call. Instead of avoiding Gowri, what Lakshmi needs to do is to send thought forms to Gowri as many number of times till she becomes comfortable saying within herself that she has returned Gowri's money on a date falling next week. **Please notice here that when Lakshmi sends the thought forms, she would be sending it as if she has already returned the money to Gowri, though the date quoted is a future date.** Then Lakshmi would call her up to say that she needs time of one week to repay her loan. Gowri would respond very positively to Lakshmi's request as Lakshmi's thought forms would have already reached her without her knowledge. You may try it out!

The best way to communicate very important information to our family members is to send the thought forms before we actually speak to them. This helps in clear and easier communication. But remember one thing. There is something called 'Law of Universe' in operation, which never aids illegal, unethical things. **Hence, any thought forms to harm some one will never work. Only positive thought forms work.**

Let us quote a real life example now. Geetha's son was a brilliant boy who had scored 100 percent in Mathematics in PUC and had joined an engineering college to do his B.E. He failed in Mathematics in the first semester. He did not take the exam when he was in the second semester as this exam was on the same day at a different timing with another subject of second year in which he was highly interested. He could not continue and had to stay at home for one year as he had not cleared Mathematics of first semester. When this information was revealed at home, all hell broke loose. He became a rebel and nobody could talk to him. Geetha tried all methods possible to counsel him, but failed. In desperation, he went and joined a call centre which promised a pay of Rs. 11,000 per month to him. He started saying that he can take care of his life and there is no need for any one to bother about him at all. **At this point, she was advised to stop scolding him and picking up fight for every small thing. She was asked to send thought forms continuously saying that he has completed his B.E. in distinction and has been placed well in a reputed company with a decent job.** She was also asked to send the thought forms that he has quit the call centre job. After 15 days, the call centre gave a test to the boy and he failed in it. He started saying that those kinds of jobs were not for a bright and intelligent boy like him. Geetha got confidence about sending thought forms and she was encouraged to write them repeatedly, after that incident. Today that boy is working in an MNC after completing B.E. with distinction.

James Allen says ***'Mind is the master weaver, both of the inner garment of character and outer garment of circumstance, and that, as they may have hitherto woven in ignorance and pain, they may now weave in enlightenment and happiness'.***

EXERCISE 2

Opposite Thinking

This is a secret of a happy and cheerful life. We are aware that our sub-conscious mind is non-judgmental. It takes whatever we feed it, without knowing as to what we are feeding is right or wrong. ***This principle is made use of, for feeding our mind with positive thoughts when we are feeling disturbed, depressed or negative.***

If we are feeling extremely tired, we have to keep telling ourselves that we are feeling energetic several times to enable our sub-conscious mind to release energy in the body and make us energetic. If we are feeling dejected and depressed, we have to continuously say that we are happy. Sub-conscious mind ensures the release of certain chemicals in the body which keeps us happy. **Try this amazing technique and be happy, always.**

This technique is extremely useful when we are facing worries, tensions or guilt. Despite our best efforts, negative thoughts keep coming to our mind making us scared, depressed and dejected. **We need to accept once for all that whatever has happened cannot be changed** and prepare our mind with positive strategies to undo the damage done or expected to befall on us.

Thus, just by thinking right opposite to negative thoughts, we become positive!

CONCEPT

3

Our Mental Mapping

From our childhood, we would have fed ideas about ourselves and about others into our mind. As we grow up it would have formed a mental map which determines its opinion about a person or situation. If the map is not reviewed and corrected from time to time, the life would continue, based on the original mapping only.

The mapping has to be such that we believe that we are perfect, whole and complete. We can achieve anything we want in life. We are always winners. We attract the right talent all the time. If the mapping is on the positive note, life will be successful. But if the mapping since childhood is based on bad experiences like feeling inadequate, failing always, fit for nothing, etc., it becomes very difficult at a later point of time to change the mental mapping.

It is important to review our mental mapping from time to time. If we notice that we have some shortcomings, we have to make a note of it and work towards changing our mental mapping. A good mentor can help us in achieving this task. A person can grow from a gross level to refined level and to move on towards more refinement, based on correction of mental mapping.

Having understood that each one of us has a hidden strength, we need to start thinking about specific goals, which can be achieved through this energy. For leading a successful life, we need to list out the essential items. When we sit for this task, our mind is generally filled with all kinds of problems. We have to get over this negativity and replace it with positive vibrations. We must understand as to what our specific goals in life are and how we would like to achieve them. Our action and thought have to be in tune with this image of ourselves. As we strengthen our belief in these thoughts, we attract cosmic energy to these vibrations, which ultimately turn it into reality.

Right from childhood, we develop our own self-image. For example, I am good or bad, I can do or cannot, I am efficient or useless. If we have a positive self-image, we automatically achieve success in life. But if we nurse negative image, our entire life is filled with pain and suffering. Hence, **unless we have a clear blueprint about "what am I", we may not be able to think clearly because our thinking is adulterated by our self-image which may not be true.** We form opinion about our self, based on what others think or tell about us. We rarely question these opinions and accept them as true. We never question as to how we developed this image for our self. Nor do we try to improve this image by 'auto-suggestion', such as 'I am capable of achieving anything in life and nothing is impossible for me.'

There is a difference between what we are and what we do. Although we may be as complete, perfect and flawless as the universe, yet what we may be doing may not be flawless. The ego within us may not allow us to be our real self. Yet having done something wrong should not make us believe that we are not capable of doing the right things. Hence, if we go on reinforcing the real qualities of self, we can get over the temporary temptations and pitfalls. If we start appreciating our universal quality then our ego will not corrupt our self-image. We will be able to send the positive thought vibrations about our completeness, perfection, flawlessness, etc. Such vibrations would lead to the right and perfect action not just for ourselves but for those around us as well.

Remember only the lesson from the experience and not the experience.

Our past is not our future. Normally we remember only the experiences that we go through and not the lesson from the experience. We have heard people saying that they can never forget some experience they have gone through somewhere in the past. Those experiences remain heavily inside and the memory of the experience harasses a person. So it becomes important to carry only the lesson learnt from that experience into our memory and not the experience itself. If somebody hurts us, the person who intended to hurt us forgets all about it after the incident but we carry it with us all along and every time we remember that incident we continue to get hurt. When we remember a person we should remember the good qualities about the person and not an incident in which they had said something to us, though that comment would have helped us in the long-run.

WE CANNOT PLEASE EVERYONE

Generally we try to please everyone else other than ourselves. But it is a fact of life that we cannot please everyone. Pleasing oneself does not make our ego bigger and bigger by the day but removes the egoistic tendency by understanding the internal growth. We all try to get influenced by some film stars or sports stars or any star of our liking and behave like them. We lead our life pleasing our spouse, our children, parents, etc. **But the success will be ours only if we learn to live the life as we like ourselves, without trying to please others.** There is an interesting anecdote. Once a man meets God after his death in heaven. God asks that man as to how he lived his life on earth. That man says that he was truthful like Sathya Harischandra, he was a donor like Karna, and starts explaining to God as to how he lived like someone else emulating their qualities. At the end, God asks him as to when did he live life like himself.

WE HAVE THE AUTHORITY WITHIN OURSELVES

People get deceived easily because they do not exercise the authority they have within themselves. Even a hypnotizer cannot hypnotize his subject if the subject does not agree for it. **Nobody can hurt us without our permission.** Then why do people get hurt easily and why do they get deceived by others? It is because they are not aware that they have all the power within themselves and they are very important. They consider others more important than themselves.

We should learn to live in this world and not allow the world to live within us. Water should be used for the boat to float on it but the water should not enter the boat. If the water enters the boat, the boat will sink. Similarly, every one, whom we come across, should be allowed to play their role from outside and they should not be allowed get inside us and start taking decisions for us. We may not be able to change the outside world but we can certainly change the world inside us. If we do this, no situation can trouble us. Merely by changing the house and the interiors of the house, we cannot be happy. If we are happy inside, we can be happy in any type of house.

OUR BELIEFS MAY BE OUR LIMITATIONS OR PRECURSORS OF GROWTH

Various beliefs that are fed into our sub-conscious mind may be our limitations. There is a difference between value and the principle. The values may change based on our belief system but the principles are eternal and cannot change. One may grow up with a belief that eating after sunset is bad and will cause harm and hence practices it all his life. Any belief which may be due to some custom may have become a practice over a period of time but it may not be true scientifically. The digestive system does not refuse to digest the food that is eaten after sunset but just because one believes that it causes harm, it actually does!

As per the custom, one may believe that one has to marry only within one's own close relative circle but scientifically one should not marry within blood relatives, as there could be health challenges in the next generation.

If over the generations, one believes that a girl has to stay at home and there is no need to study, it is only a belief and not the truth. If a girl is given an opportunity to study and grow, she would do it without any doubt. Initially she may face some challenges because she is also fed with the belief that a girl is not meant to go out for study.

A belief that a girl who dresses up in modern clothes is not a good choice for marriage is only a belief based on what is fed into our minds over a period of time but it is not true. A girl in modern clothes can actually become the best life partner.

Whatever we feed into our sub-conscious mind over a period of time may become our beliefs and may limit our growth if the belief is not of positive nature. If we are fed with positive beliefs like 'I will remember whatever I have read when it is needed', 'I am always a winner', 'I can do anything that is assigned to me well', etc. will ensure that we can achieve whatever we want. It is important to note here that negative input and negative beliefs will be acting as our limitations whereas positive inputs will act as precursors for our growth and development.

OUTSIDE WORLD IS A MIRROR REFLECTION OF OUR INSIDE WORLD

If we feel very confident with our preparation for the examination, we see the outside world also with all preparedness. We feel happy to take the examination. If we have not prepared well, we see the chaos everywhere as is experienced in our mind. If we are internally very happy, we can participate in a marriage function with joy but if we are sad inside, any amount of celebration outside will not make us happy. **So it is important that we find a solution to our problems within ourselves first before looking outside.** If our thoughts are centered on fear, we face only fearful situations. If our thoughts are positive and focused on a solution, the solution is visible outside.

WE ARE ALWAYS RIGHT

Henry Ford has said ***'If you think you can, if you think you cannot, both the times you are right'.*** If we consciously think that we cannot achieve anything in life and feed the same to our sub-conscious mind continuously, our sub-conscious mind believes it to be true and ensures that we would not achieve anything worthwhile in our life. If our conscious mind thinks that we can achieve whatever we want to achieve, our sub-conscious mind believes it to be true and manifests that. So it is important to feed the right ideas into our sub-conscious mind. **Our sub-conscious mind works like an auto-pilot.** If the auto pilot is planned for east and we are steering the plane to the north with our hand, the auto-pilot goes back to the east only.

If we notice in a circus, small elephants are tied to well fastened anchor rod with a strong iron chain whereas grown up big elephants are tied with a thin rope to a small anchor point. It is because the elephants when they are young, try very hard to escape. After some trials they come to know that they cannot escape. So they stop trying as they believe that they cannot escape. **Our sub-conscious mind believes what we have fed into it and stops making any effort after some time.** We call it as ***comfort zone***. If some one is struggling for money and after a few futile attempts to earn good money, stops believing in himself and feels comfortable in being poor, it becomes difficult to convince him that it is possible for him to come out of his poverty. A boy who has been continuously scoring only 40% marks remains in the comfort zone of scoring only 40% and does not want to work hard to score more.

HOW TO GET BELIEF IN OURSELVES?

The most important thing is to believe that we are extraordinary and we are successful and significant people. As children we gave shape to our thoughts in the form of pictures. Then we learnt to express our emotions through words. Then we learnt to speak and then visualize a picture of what we have spoken. **When we think, a neuron is**

formed in the brain. Every experience we undergo, gets stored as a neuron in the brain initially and then as a memory in the sub-conscious mind. Our behaviour most of the time will be based on the previous experiences stored in the form of memories. This is the reason why children born to same parents despite getting the same experience behave differently, as each perceives it differently and stores it in his memory. **The memory gradually becomes a belief system.**

The memory stored in our sub-conscious mind is not the result of a single experience. It will be a series of experiences which will super impose upon one another. Whenever a similar situation arises, the conscious mind immediately gets the earlier input from the memory bank of our sub-conscious mind. If we have fed our experiences which were totally opposing one another, there will be a lot of confusion in our sub-conscious mind and we experience confusion in our thinking and action. So it becomes important to **keep checking what we have fed and remove the unwanted stuff with Unburden exercise and feed what is relevant and important to us, to be successful.** Let us do an experiment. Take a vessel full of water. Keep adding small pebbles into the vessel. You will notice that with the introduction of every pebble, some water goes out. At some point of time, all the water may be replaced by the pebbles. The pebbles are the inputs we keep giving to ourselves. The input that we give may remove the belief that we already have. If we have a goal of becoming a good singer, then the pebble that we put within ourselves should be a good musical CD, a role model of a good music teacher, attending musical concerts, etc. The pebbles must be carefully selected so that it strengthens our positive beliefs.

EXERCISE

3

Unburden Exercise

So far we have understood the importance of our sub-conscious mind. Sub-conscious mind is our best friend and we should learn to make use of it. Our sub-conscious mind is filled with experiences, both good and bad. We would have filled it with pain, anger, disappointment, agony, and many more negative feelings which keep coming up and tormenting us. **It is time to stop and clean our sub-conscious mind to enable us to move forward.**

What we need to do is to sit comfortably with lots of paper, pen, an empty earthen pot and a match box. We should take time to remember all the incidents since our childhood, which are lodged in the sub-conscious mind causing us pain. We should write it down on a piece of paper, then fold the paper and put it in the empty earthen pot. Once we feel relieved, we may burn all the papers with a lighted match stick. **This exercise of writing away hidden pains on the paper and burning it off is called unburdening.** This has to be done on a regular basis to become free and light headed and light hearted. Once we are sure that we have unburdened all the negative feelings that are causing pain, we can get prepared to learn about the principles of success consciousness.

CONCEPT

4

Success is a Journey

'Success is progressive realization of a worthwhile Dream' says Earl Nightingale in his famous 'Strangest Secret' audio tape. One has to have a goal of achieving one's dream with a time frame and work diligently towards it. As we have already seen, thoughts lead us to action and fulfil our dreams. Each and every step that we take to reach our goal is success. Success is not only what we achieve at the end. It is experienced at every step that we take in reaching our goal. No one reaches the goal without working for it.

Edmond Hilary and Tensing Norvey were the first to scale Himalayas after a long struggle. Every step they climbed was taking them towards their goal of reaching the top of Himalayas. Bhimsen Joshi became a noted singer after practicing for endless hours on a daily basis. Daily deliberate action and success in the daily practice led him to achieve the pinnacle of success.

There is no shortcut to success. If some one tries to become successful overnight, he will not be able to sustain the success. As he would not have grown on the journey to success, his fall would also be sudden and recovery from it may take its own time. It takes effort, focus and dedication to become successful. Success obtained by illegal means will not remain for long. As Gandhiji says, "means is as important as the end in becoming successful." ***Message that the society gets, when one becomes successful, has far reaching consequences than the person who became successful.***

Failures should not deter us, as failures are just a bend and not the end of the road to success. For preventing such bends, we need to mark our milestones and achieve them in the form of inner victories.

CONCEPT

5

Inner Victory

It is very important to strive for inner victory under any circumstances. Working for small inner victories, prepares us for achieving big steps later in life. By not being true to ourselves, we invite failures. For example, if we have told some one that we would be meeting them at a particular time, but do not keep up our word, it is internal failure. **Here our sub-conscious mind receives a message that is ok not to honor our word. It starts believing that we can say one thing but do another thing.** Next time if we try to give an appointment to some one, it ensures that we don't keep up our appointment which leads to our internal failure.

If we decide to get up at 5 am the next day, when the alarm rings, don't ever say that you will get up later after 10 or 15 minutes. By doing so we would be feeding our sub-conscious mind with the information that it is alright not to do what we have decided earlier.

If we do not take inner victory seriously, we can never have private victory and public victory later in our lives. It is important to ensure each and every time to mean and do what we say, to attain internal victory.

CONCEPT

6

SWOT Analysis

This technique is extremely useful for achieving the 'inner victory'. **We all know how to use SWOT analysis in all our projects but we may not know that using it on a daily basis in our life has far reaching impact.** This technique helps us to evaluate ourselves at the closing of each day in order to understand how we have behaved during the day and what impact it can have on our success. Daily personal analysis will prepare us to become better human beings. **It is both corrective and preventive**. Let us look at the SWOT analysis in detail.

S Stands for Strength

First we need to know our strengths. Being a good communicator, a good listener, hard working enough to finish any given task, lending a helping hand, are some examples of our personal strengths. When we go through the events which happened during the day, we can know where we have exhibited our strengths and where we failed to exhibit our strengths. If we can objectively analyze this, it becomes easier for us to correct ourselves and enable us to exhibit our strength, whenever it is necessary.

W Stands for Weakness

Poor communication skills, not listening to what others say, not finishing any given task, laziness, quick tempered behaviour, forgetfulness, recklessness, rashness, etc are some of our personal weaknesses. When we analyze the events of the day, wherever we have exhibited our weakness, it is to be noted and analyzed in order to fix the weakness. If we start analyzing it on a daily basis, the habit of exhibiting weakness gradually gets reduced.

O Stands for Opportunity

We do not notice opportunities as they pass by us on a daily basis when we do not keep an open mind. We tend to miss the opportunity of talking to a scientist or an interesting person although we are in his company during the day. We let go the opportunity to prove that we are good speakers by not preparing well for the occasion, we let go of the opportunity to prove our point by not documenting whatever we are doing, we miss the opportunity by being skeptic to new ideas coming from others, we let go of the opportunity of sorting out the misunderstandings, we let go of the opportunity of working hard now to have a bright future in the long-run, etc. We can learn to identify the missed opportunities on a daily basis so that we do not repeat the same mistakes next day.

T Stands for Threats

If we look at the events of the day and spot the situation which may become a major threat, it becomes easier to take remedial action or not committing that same error again. One of our colleague could be a threat to us with whom we confide our personal matters and he or she discusses with others added with own version. Some family member could be a threat to us by projecting us in bad light. Our own communication not conveyed properly could lead to misunderstandings and could precipitate matters, thereby becoming a threat. An important work if procrastinated could result in a threat of losing one's reputation. Improper home work before a meeting could become a threat of losing a contract. Not communicating one's love could result in threat of losing him or her in marriage. Assuming certain things about a friend can result in a threat of losing friendship, etc.

SWOT Analysis on a daily basis prepares us to become sensitive and refined in our actions, which lead to success. Hence we need to fix our 'goals' and the 'strengths' which shall be used by us, through mental mapping.

CONCEPT

7

How to Set a Goal?

Goal setting is a science. It is a science because properly set goals can be achieved and documented. There is a S.M.A.R.T.E.R way of setting goals.

S—Specific

Goals are personal. So goals will have to be very specific. It should not be vague. If we say 'I want to become a great writer', then it is not a specific goal. We should be specific in saying 'my goal is to write one non-fiction book of 300 pages this year'. Specific goals give a sense of direction to work on.

M—Measurable

If the goal is to write a book of 300 pages this year, measuring how many pages one is doing as the time is passing, would keep us focused and motivated to complete the task in the given time. Planning a milestone to be achieved in a day, depending on the available time would help.

A—Action-centered

Any goal that is set has to be followed up by action. If

there is no time for action, then setting a goal is meaningless. Thoughts must lead to action to realize one's goal. For a book of 300 pages, one should act by writing atleast a page a day.

R—Realistic

If one cannot devote even one hour a day for writing, then setting a goal of writing a book of 300 pages in a year may not be achievable. We should never set goals for failure. Once a realistic goal is set and achieved, it enhances our self-confidence. At the same time, the goal should not be set too low, else our full potential will not be exploited.

T—Time Bound

If a time frame is not fixed for any goal, it will not fructify at all and we get into the habit of procrastinating. There will be no charm in having a goal without a target date. The target date fixed sets the action by the universe into motion to make it happen.

E—Exciting

The process of achieving the goal must be exciting. We should look forward to the process with a lot of excitement which will help us in accomplishing our goal easily.

R—Rewarding

Every goal that we fix and achieve must be rewarded. Small rewards for small goals and big rewards for big goals are recommended.

Thinking a goal through

When we are thinking about how to achieve our goals, asking the following questions can help us to focus on the sub-goals that lead to their achievement:

- What skills do I need to achieve this?
- What information and knowledge do I need?
- What help, assistance, or collaboration do I need?
- What resources do I need?
- What can block my progress?
- Am I making any assumptions?

There are several ways of making our goals work. By experience we have found that ***there is a higher degree of probability to stick to one's goal, if we learn to include as many of our senses as possible, to help us along.***

One of the methods is called **Emotional Freedom Technique (EFT).** EFT is often used to change our emotional reaction to a certain situation. For instance, if we get nervous while speaking in front of people, we can learn to use EFT to make affirmations (which will be discussed in detail later) and tap oneself on specific points of the body. EFT is nicknamed "tapping" because we actually do tap ourselves repeatedly at specific spots as we are saying the sentences we construct about our goal—the change we desire.

There is another method to make our goal work. It is often called **VAK, which stands for Visual/Auditory/Kinesthetic.** If we are engaged in our work with our heart, soul, mind and body—and we are sure to be quite successful! So, to set a goal and put the power of VAK behind it, here's what you do:

1. Write your goal down.
2. Close your eyes, and ask yourself ***"what will you visualize to know that you've attained your goal?"*** Take a breath or two, and see what pictures you get to see when your goal is achieved. You will probably get more than one vision. Open your eyes, and write each of them down.
3. Again, close your eyes and ask yourself ***"what will people say to you once you've reached the goal?"*** After you've recorded your answer, try asking yourself "what will people say about you once you've reached your goal?" And finally, ask what you would say to yourself when your goal is reached. Record your answers.
4. Now, close your eyes again. Ask yourself, ***"how would you feel when you've reached this new goal."*** Take some time to let this sink in, and see what feelings arise in you. Once you have a good strong feeling going, ask yourself about the color,

shape, texture, and even the temperature of that feeling. Finally, ask yourself where the feeling is located in your body. Record all your answers. Don't rush yourself; give yourself time to really get into the feeling of reaching this goal.

5. Finally, ask yourself, ***"what belief you could state about yourself that will help you get this goal."*** For instance, if you want to lose weight but always snack at night, could you create a belief about yourself that you are able to easily turn your attention from eating after 7:00 PM? Work on this replacing your current belief that it is "impossible not to eat" or "I must eat because I get too fatigued, too bored, or too scared not to eat at night." In other words, replace your negative self-talk with a positive belief in yourself as someone who is capable of doing what you want to do.
6. ***Be sure to ask yourself if you foresee any reason NOT to reach this goal.*** If you secretly think that being thinner will be bad in some way you will not reach your goal until you have removed that belief. We always have a secret reason for what we don't want to do vis-a-vis what we say we want to do. I say I want to improve my English speaking skills, but secretly I don't want to put in the extra half an hour a day to do that. So, of course, I don't! I say I want to quit smoking but in my heart of hearts, I do not wish to lose the momentary pleasure that I get from each puff. Bring your secret reasons up into your consciousness, and you'll go a long way to helping yourself get that goal.

The point here is to create a framework around you that helps support you in all your senses. If you have a goal to grow a rose garden, you can close your eyes and envision the layout, the sunshine, the colors, and the smells for sure. The more you can embody your goals, the more you'll be able to make it stick. Try it and send us your feedback.

Why should we set Goals?

1. **Direction:** Without even the smallest of goals, it is easy to feel as though we lack direction or feel lost. Having goals focuses our energy and enables us to work towards something we value.
2. **Individual Purpose:** Goals, whether big or small, are vitally important to give us individuality and purpose. Goals can be personal, social, political...anything that you find important to you and your life. Goals are unique to you and your needs, wishes, desires and dreams, and so, YOU decide what they should be.
3. **Boosting Self-Esteem:** Without goals we don't have accomplishments. Every time you set a goal and reach it, you prove to yourself that you are capable of achieving what you set out to achieve. This results in a natural boost to our self-esteem and a deeper belief in oneself.
4. **Positive Reinforcement:** When we accomplish our goals, we reinforce our belief in ourselves to set and accomplish new ones. This helps to muffle negativity, doubt and fear, making way for a "can do" attitude that helps us continue to strive.
5. **Reaching our Full Potential:** Goals enable us to move beyond our comfort zone and become as best as we can be. They allow us to take-on new and exciting challenges and help us grow as individuals.

Some of the **stepping stones of success** are as follows:

- We should learn to be positively different from others.
- When others are in doubt we should show confidence.
- When others refuse to take up any work, we should come forward and take responsibilities.
- When others act cowardly, we should exhibit courage.

- When others give up, we should take up with determination.
- Instead of daydreaming we should act with a vision and a mission.
- With the above qualities, we can lead a life of happiness and prosperity not just for ourselves but also for others.

Adding Quality to our Time

Another important aspect of goal setting is to know our priorities and work. But most of the time, we are not aware as to how we should fix our priorities. The following story is a good eye opener in knowing priorities. When things in your life seem almost too much to handle, when 24 hours in a day is not enough, remember the story of a jar and 2 cups of coffee.

A professor stood before his philosophy class and had some items in front of him. When the class began, wordlessly, he picked up a very large and empty jar and proceeded to fill it with golf balls. He then asked the students if the jar was full. They agreed that it was. The professor then picked up a box of pebbles and poured them into the jar. He shook the jar lightly. The pebbles rolled into the open areas between the golf balls. He then asked the students again if the jar was full. They agreed it was. The professor next picked up a box of sand and poured it into the jar. Of course, the sand filled up everything else. He asked once more if the jar was full. The students responded with a unanimous "yes." The professor then produced two cups of coffee from under the table and poured the entire contents into the jar, effectively filling the empty space between the sand. The students laughed. "Now," said the professor, as the laughter subsided, "I want you to recognize that this jar represents your life. **The golf balls are the important things—God, family, children, health, friends, and Favorite passions**—things that if everything else was lost and only they remained, your life would still be full. The pebbles are the other things that matter like your job, house, and car. The sand is everything else — the small stuff. "If you put the sand into the jar first," he continued, "there is no room for the pebbles or the golf balls. The same goes for life. If you spend all your time and energy on the small stuff, you will never have room for the things that are important to you.

So... **Pay attention to the things that are critical to your happiness**. Play With your children. Take time to get medical checkups. Take your partner out to dinner. There will always be time to clean the house and fix the disposal. "Take care of the golf balls first — the things that really matter. Set your priorities. The rest is just sand." One of the students raised her hand and inquired what the coffee represented. The professor smiled. "I'm glad you asked". It just goes to show you that no matter how full your life may seem, there's always room for a couple of cups of coffee with a friend."

Why do we fail?

We set our goals because we want to be successful but many times we fail. We have to analyze the reasons for our failure. It could be any of the following:

- We suggest to ourselves strongly that we cannot achieve this goal and believe it to be true.
- We focus only on our shortcomings and not our strengths.
- We keep comparing ourselves with more successful people and feel that we are not like them to be able to achieve success.
- We feel sad because we feel that luck is not favoring us.
- We get into the habit of going to the temples and imagining that God will fulfil our goals without doing anything on our part.
- We keep remembering only the failures we have experienced and affirm to ourselves that we are born to fail and we cannot change.
- We do not focus on every step of achieving our goal but we expect successful results.
- We are happy competing with others but not working complimentarily with one another.

- Our ego comes in the way of knowing our weaknesses and working on improving it.
- Our negative attitude prevents us from observing and appreciating good work done by others.
- Our arrogance prevents learning from others and implementing the same in our life.
- We cannot face criticism with a smile. If one learns to smile despite adverse circumstances, the steps to success become easier and enjoyable.

EXERCISE

Fish Bone Analysis

Most often we do not give a serious thought to our 'threats' or problems. We do not try to analyze its root cause nor try to find the suitable solution for the same. As a result, our small little problems become unmanageably big and make us feel miserable. On the contrary if we try to tackle our present problem and list out various means to solve them we will be able to resolve them successfully.

Please examine the picture given below which shows a fish with all the bones on its body. Let us use this picture for analyzing our problems.

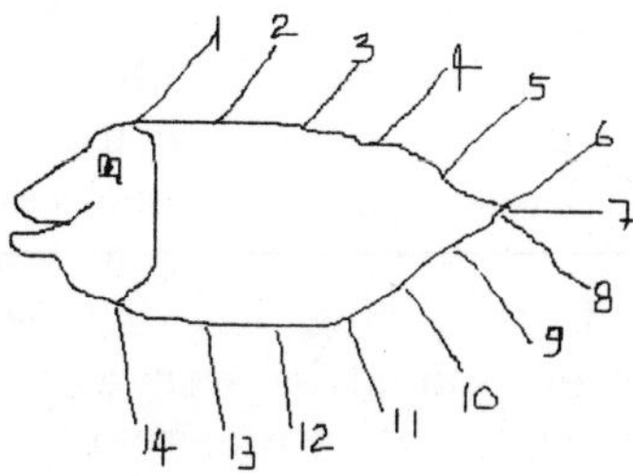

Fish-1

Whenever we encounter problems we should try to go to its root cause and face it one by one. **Once we have tackled the root of the problem then the same problem does not bother us again.** Let us take an example of Arpita who is working in an office. Everyday she is late in reaching office and therefore gets scolded by her superiors. This is the first and central bone of the fish representing her basic problem. The other bones are analyzed by asking questions as given below:

1. Why does she get late everyday?

   Ans: Because she misses the bus.
2. Why does she miss her bus for the office?

   Ans: Because, she is not able to reach Bus Stop on time.
3. Why doesn't she reach the bus stop on time?

   Ans: Because of delay due to other household works.
4. Why this delay?

   Ans: Because she is unable to get up early in the morning.
5. Why?

   Ans: Because she sleeps late in the night.
6. Why?

   Ans: Because she watches late night shows in the TV.

Here we have reached at the root of the problem and now we can also find the solution. **Is watching TV till late night as important as the work schedule next day?** Because of one wrong habit, she is suffering for the whole day, day-by-day. If only she leaves this habit she would be having ample time for all the household chores as well as the office work. Thus, instead of getting lost in the whirlpool of problems, the problems should be seen as a whole like the bones of the fish shown in the picture below. Now the bones, no longer pinch like the first picture and instead helps in smooth floating even in the turbulent waters.

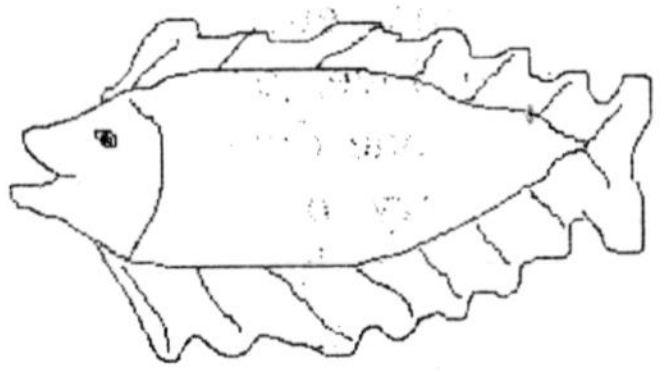

Fish-2

Remaining with the problem without finding its solution, precipitates the problem further. **It is better to go into 'solution mode' as early as possible**. Once we are in the solution mode, not one but many roads to recover appear. Please pick up your biggest problem, say smoking habit and do a fish bone analysis.

Problem-solving can be facilitated by observing and learning from the Universe around us. Nature is the best teacher and if we work in harmony with nature we are sure to succeed in all our ventures.

Fish-2

Remaining with the problem without finding its [illegible] the problem multiplies. It is better to go into solution mode as early as possible. Once we are in the solution mode, not one but many modes to recover [illegible]. Please pick up your biggest problem say smoking habit and do a fish bone analysis.

Problem solving can be facilitated by observing and learning from the Universe around us. Nature is the best teacher and if we work in harmony with nature we are sure to succeed in all our ventures.

CONCEPT

8

Applying the Laws of Universe for Success

Human beings are integral part of the universe, wherein, the super conscious resides. We may have made many inventions and discoveries but we have not been able to conquer the universe. There is something which is far more superior to all of us. We must acknowledge the fact that we are a small fraction of the entire universe. ***Since the universe is a complete, flawless and perfect system, so are we.*** Just as each drop in an ocean has the same qualities of the entire ocean, each one of us possesses the unlimited energy that is possessed by the universe. We have to understand the principles of the Universe and take the best advantage of it for our growth and progress. Let us see how we can use the principles of nature to draw this unlimited energy for achieving success.

The principles of the Universe are impersonal. The laws

of nature do not vary with caste, creed, colour, riches or poverty, intellect or foolishness, men or women, fat or thin, small or big, etc. The nature gives us these bounties to the extent we take them. **This is called the law of infinity**. Sun is always present during the day with its light and heat, irrespective of the position of any person, be it a poor man or a rich man, white or black, educated or illiterate. ***He who sits inside a dark room and blames the sun for not giving him the sunlight should instead blame himself for not coming out in the sun or for not opening the windows to let the sunlight in.*** Similarly, the water continuously flows in the river. We may choose to take a dip into it and enjoy the freshness. Another person may prefer to sit beside the river and shed tears on his failures. Another person may be inspired to sing beside the river. Another depressed soul may jump into it and commit suicide. None of these actions affect the flow of water in the river. It is up to us whether to collect one spoonful of water from the river to quench our thirst or take a pot full for satisfying many other thirsts.

The nature has abundant resources for everyone and it grows by leaps and bounds. For example; do we know how many grains one-wheat seed can yield or how many apples can we have from an apple tree? We can reap abundance and prosperity by nurturing nature and not harming nature. Nature provides many resources for our well-being. In return, we are expected to do good to nature and others. Goodness never goes wasted. The results may not be immediately visible but accumulate in our account and come to us when we need them most. **This is the law of seed or increasing returns.**

Another principle of the Universe is the **'Law of Cause and Effect'**. The thought, belief and the emotion that we display is the cause and we see the effect because of them. Can we expect a mango tree from a neem seed? What we sow, so we reap. If we sow Papaya seedling, can we expect Mangoes to be reaped. Whatever we sow, we have to reap its fruits only. Our feelings, thoughts and beliefs, which reside within us, are the cause for the effects, which are visible to us in the form of our behaviour. Hence, it is very important to carefully select our thoughts so that we get the desirable results. Right action leads to right results. ***Inaction will lead to decay and death.***

The human body consists of various parts and systems which are unique and work in perfect harmony with each other. Thus cooperation is the nature's way of doing things. **This is called the law of constructive Competition.** Competition, comparison or confrontation, are unnatural phenomena. The human beings need not work against each other for success but try to mobilize synergy for great results. Nature or Universe never asks anyone to compete to use its resources. It gives its resources equally to everyone. We feel that we have to compete in every area of life but competition kills creativity. Most of the times, the victory of a person is based on studying the weaknesses of his opponent. ***Competition should be within oneself to improve one's own performance every time.*** Even in a competition, if the focus of the participant is to do his best, he would be a winner. If he is fed with the information that his opponent is strong, he concedes defeat in his mind even before he plays his game. Instead of competition, if there is cooperation, it can lead to our own creativity getting better every time.

Though each one of us is unique, there is something common in all living beings which inter-connects all of us with each other. If we try to harm others by our thoughts, words or actions, we first harm ourselves. For example; by getting angry with others, we lose our hormonal balance and also physical happiness. Giving happiness to others alone will make us happy. **This is called the law of universal inter-connectivity.**

Nothing in nature is absolutely good or bad. There is a balance between the good and the bad, the positive and the negative. Only when the balance is disturbed due to excess or deficit of any component, we feel the turbulence. Waves are inspiring not because they rise and fall, but because every time they fall, they never fail to rise again. Human life also has a balance-sheet where total assets equal total liabilities. Therefore, we should refrain from indulging in excesses of any kind. **This is called the law of complementarity.**

Nothing in this world is permanent. The seasons change, the age brings in changes from childhood to old age, our beliefs, attitudes, behaviours change from time to time. No one is permanently lucky or unlucky. The rich can become poor and *vice-versa*. Yet we all resist the change and take our own time to accept it. Rather than accepting the changes from outside, we can bring desirable changes from within and set an example for others. This is called the **law of inevitability of change.**

The time waits for none and once lost, is gone forever. **This is called the law of supremacy of time.** Since we have no control over the past or the future, we should learn to live in the present. Life has no pause buttons. Time has no holiday. Dreams have no expiry date! Since we cannot hold on to the time, we can certainly use it in the best possible manner and realize our dreams. Please appreciate how beautifully we get one more day added to our life, not just for ourselves but many others who need us.

We need to understand these laws of nature and use them to our advantage. With a firm conviction in these laws, we need to mould our thoughts and beliefs in the direction of achieving our goals. Now we would like to share our experiments, in creating our own future. We have a request before we start. We want all of you to use our research and our findings on how to become successful in life by having an open mind, just as an opened parachute is useful during the dive from an aeroplane and not an unopened one!

CONCEPT

Success-conscious Learning—The Seven 'C's

Every successful person has a painful story.
Every painful story has a successful ending.

Accept the pain and get ready for success.

There is some learning drawn from the laws of universe to be implemented for becoming successful in life. **It is important to believe that we are part of the perfect, whole and complete Universe and hence possess the same qualities.** It is important to believe that we are capable of facing any situation and we will come out as winners. Once these beliefs take their root in our sub-conscious mind, it is easy to become what we want to become. By doing so, we can start attracting wealth, health, happiness and prosperity. Let us learn what beliefs to nurture and what to uproot, one by one. These are described as seven 'C's. The first C is Control.

Control

The law of infinity teaches that we have an infinite potential lying dormant within us, yet we do not use it optimally. One of the major inhibiting factor is the tendency to control others or be controlled by others. We all feel that exercising control is a natural phenomenon and there is nothing wrong with it. Parents try to control children, children control parents, teachers control students, students control teachers, boss controls subordinates, subordinates control the boss ....Every one tries to control everyone else, yet feels quite helpless. We have to understand that controlling does not help. **We need to lead and not control.**

What is Locus of Control?

Locus of control means where you place the power to influence, how you feel about yourself and others. It is important to determine if the locus of control is external or internal to figure out if you are susceptible to being controlled by others.

External Locus of Control

External locus of control is giving other people, places, and things the power to influence your feelings about yourself. External locus of control places approval, recognition, acceptance, reinforcement, and affirmation of self-worth into the hands of other people, places, and things. ***Unless others approve, recognize, accept, reinforce, or affirm your worth, then you feel worthless, non-approved, unrecognized, not accepted, and non-reinforced.*** This makes you susceptible to being controlled by others' thinking, emotions, and actions.

Internal Locus of Control

Internal locus of control is giving yourself the power to influence your feelings about yourself. ***Internal locus of control places self-approval, self-recognition, self-acceptance, self-reinforcement, and self-affirmation of worth into your own hands.*** In this way it is only up to you and your own efforts at self-love and care, to feel worthwhile, valuable, competent, skillful, creative, knowledgeable and capable of living your life for yourself and not controlled by others. You

What are some Myths and Realities about Control?

Sl. No.	*Myths*	*Realities*
1	*2*	*3*
1.	The more I exercise control on others, the more control I'll have in life.	Because others are free to accept or reject your control, the resulting dynamic tension between the controlled and controller creates a circumstance in life which is more out of control than you first desired. The more you let go of control over others, the more control you will have over your internal locus of control.
2.	I am not controlling people when I am helping them or trying to fix things for them.	You are controlling them because when you are fixing or helping them and they are not taking personal responsibility and control of their own lives.
3.	If I manipulate others to do what I want them to do, this is not amounting to controlling them.	You are influencing them to do what you want. So they are not doing things out of their own free will. Instead you are deciding for them.
4.	I am not controlling others if they are unintentionally intimidated by me and go along with what I want them to do.	If you are unintentionally placed in an external locus of control position by others, they have put you in a position of power over them. You are in control over them even though you are not aware of this at that time.
5.	I should be in control of everything that is important in my life.	Unfortunately you are powerless to control most people, places, and things in your life. You can only be in

1	2	3
		full control of your own thoughts, emotions, and actions.
6.	I should hold on to and help the people in my life that I see are having problems in taking care of themselves in acceptable, self-responsible and self-controlling ways.	The more you try to hold on to these people, the harder they will pull away or the weaker and more dependent on you they will become. It is better to become emotionally detached from their problems and let them solve them on their own so that they still can relate to you in a free and open way.
7.	Other people will condemn me if I become detached from the people close to me.	It makes no difference what others think about you. What is important is helping the people in your life to become more responsible for their own lives.
8.	I should never let go of those things I am trying to control and change because if I do I'd be considered a failure.	Your struggle to control and change things outside your internal locus of control is going to wear you down and possibly break you. You will be healthier, happier, and more in control of your life if you let go of the uncontrollable and unchangeable in your life.
9.	If I love someone, I should always be there for them, even if they tend to become a little dependent on me for a while.	You're a person who could possibly love a person so much that you contribute to that person's inability to become self-responsible and who could possibly love a person so much that you contribute to that person's inability to become self-responsible and in self-control of life. In reality your love may

	make the person over dependent on you. Love is learning to let go of the uncontrollable and unchangeable people in your life, in self-control of life. In reality your love may make the person over dependent on you. Love is learning to let go of the uncontrollable and unchangeable people in your life.
10. When people are helpless, I should step in and take over to help them get on their feet.	People might appear helpless to you but they often have inner reserves of competence, skills, and ability to solve their own problems. If you take over their problems for them, this might disable them from being productive problem solvers and agents for their own change leading to overdependence on you.
11. When things are not going the way they should, I should take control of the situation to make it the way it's supposed to be.	You are being irrationally led by your dreams, fantasies, tradition, and promises of how life should be. In your idealism you can become so over-controlling that is counter productive.
12. I should take care of things because only then they will happen the way they are supposed to.	A caretaker works hard at being sure that everything is the way it is supposed to be for everyone. This over controlling behaviour succeeds in disabling people who are being cared for and then things are never the way they are supposed to be. You never get what you really want when you are over-controlling.

are then fully responsible for your own thinking, emotions, and actions in life.

Locus of Control is a 'Power' Issue. If you give others power over you, you overemphasize external locus of control in your life. On the other hand, if you empower yourself, you emphasize internal locus of control in your life. ***In order to handle the control issues in your life, it is better to emphasize internal locus of control so that you are able to let go of the need to control and change others and concentrate on controlling and changing yourself.***

So, from the above discussion, we can understand that one has to focus on internal locus of control to become success-conscious.

Normally disciplining is mistaken as controlling, but it is not so. Discipline is a principle of life which helps us in becoming successful. While disciplining, we try to objectively guide a person to follow societal Do's and Dont's, in larger public interest. For example, by enforcing road safely rules, we are ensuring the well-being of all the road users. Similarly, without disciplining the students, teachers can not provide quality education. On the contrary, control mechanism has a vested interest attached to it. It is exercised purely in self-interest.

EXERCISE

5

Understanding Our Tendencies and the First 'C'

Let us do some exercises to know what our tendencies are and how we can change them for being successful in life.

Need to Control: A Self-Assessment. A few statements are given below. Please put an 'X' mark next to the ones which reflect your true nature about people, places and things in your life.

S. No.	*Statement*	*X mark*
1.	If you control other people, they will do what you want them to do.	
2.	It is a way to keep everything orderly, precise, and predictable, so that you don't go crazy or insane.	
3.	You hate to be out of control or to lose your control.	
4.	If things don't go your way, you feel you'll have to work harder or have to struggle to reorganize and correct them.	
5.	You have a hard time seeing people you care for getting hurt because their lives are out of control.	

S. No.	Statement	X mark
6.	You hate to have people see your true feelings especially if they are angry, unpleasant, or negative so you struggle to control them and keep them inside you, to avoid upsetting others.	
7.	You are on the watch for being taken advantage of by others.	
8.	You are afraid of being manipulated or led into doing something you really don't want to do.	
9.	When you see something or someone who needs to be fixed, you often step in.	
10.	You came from a dysfunctional or crazy home life and you have no desire to repeat it in your current home life.	
11.	You have an image, dream, or ideal of the way things are supposed to be and you work at trying to get it to be that way.	
12.	You are afraid that if you don't take care of things, things will never get done.	
13.	You feel if 'you don't do it, then no one will.'	
14.	You are afraid that everything you have worked for will be lost, so you take control to ensure this doesn't happen.	
15.	When you feel intimidated, you compensate by taking more control of the situation.	
16.	You find it difficult not to help when you see a person or thing which appears helpless and out of control.	
17.	You tend to hold to an 'it's my way or the highway' approach with people who don't do what you want them to do. You hope this will ensure that they change their bad behaviour.	
18.	You are frightened, scared, or nervous when things seem to be crazy or out of control. So your first impulse is to take charge.	
19.	You want everybody in your immediate life to be happy and you'll do whatever it takes to make it so.	
20.	You know how hard life can be for those who go into it unprepared and unaware. So you make sure that the people you care for are not taken advantage of.	

INTERPRETATION: If you checked 'X' against 3 or more, you have a tendency to control the people, places, and things in your life.

Control Mechanisms: A Self-Assessment. Here are some *ways* in which you control people to do the things for you that you could do for yourself. Put an 'X' next to those behaviours, which are usually true for you.

S. No.	*Statement*	*X mark*
1.	You act helpless, incompetent, or lost.	
2.	You make the other person feel very important and essential in your life.	
3.	You tell them reasons (which are a lie) as to why you couldn't get things done.	
4.	You feel self-pity and act out the belief that you have done everything for everyone in your life so it's your turn now to be taken care of.	
5.	You act tense, anxious, and stressed out and incapable of caring for yourself.	
6.	You resort to threats of suicide or self-destruction to get others to care for you.	
7.	You give others a set of conditions, they must fulfil, before you will give them acceptance, care or approval.	
8.	You offer them rewards if they will do what you want to be done.	
9.	You threaten others with withdrawal of attention, support, affection, or approval if they don't do what you want to be done.	
10.	You play on their sympathy and concern by being a pathetic martyr, overworked and unappreciated victim.	
11.	You play on your physical or emotional illness, be it real or perceived, to get them to do what you want.	
12.	You play on their need to be needed to get them to take care of you.	
13.	You play up to their guilt and over responsible nature to get what you want.	
14.	You act dependent in order to give others a sense of importance and value in helping you.	
15.	You fall apart when faced with having to do something which you would rather not do.	
16.	You play up to a person who has a need to fix things that things have got so 'out of control' for you.	
17.	You promise to change or reform the behaviours the others want from you, in order to get what you want out of them, never meaning to change or reform yourself.	

S. No.	Statement	X mark
18.	When you sense another person is pulling away from you, you feign a problem or need which you believe will get that person involved with you again.	
19.	You act as if you have forgotten to do something which you know the other person will do for you.	

INTERPRETATION: If you checked 3 or more items, you overuse control mechanisms to get people to do what you could do for yourself.

To find out if others are controlling you to do things for them, which otherwise they could do for themselves, go back and put an 'X' next to those statements true for people in your life. If 3 or more are checked, then you are being over controlled by others!

Emotional Response: A Self-Assessment. Here are some ways in which you could control your emotional response to life. Put an 'X' next to the statements which are usually true for you.

S. No.	Statement	X mark
1.	You allow yourself to be free, open, and expressive to the feelings you are experiencing at the moment.	
2.	You usually do not try to hide your feelings, be they positive or negative.	
3.	You are usually able to accept the consequences of others' response to your positive or negative feelings.	
4.	You are able to freely express your anger, in an assertive confrontation mode with no raging, yelling, screaming, ranting, or raving at other people.	
5.	You do not avoid letting others know if you are angry with them and yet you don't blow your cool in the telling.	
6.	You can show enjoyment, excitement, and enthusiastic feelings when the event appropriately calls for such a response.	
7.	You are able to openly cry and grieve over a loss in your life.	
8.	You are able to do anger workouts over old, unresolved anger in your life so as to free yourself of the emotional burden and drain these repressed and unresolved feelings affecting your emotional energy.	

S. No.	*Statement*	*X mark*
9.	You are able to express your violent rage and anger outbursts privately so that you can return to people in a more composed way to let them know in a healthy assertive way how angry you are.	
10.	You are able to analyze your emotions all the time and see if they are congruent or in sync with your thinking and actions. If they are not, you are able to figure out why and what to do about it.	
11.	You do not allow self-pity to be a driving force in your attitude in order to use your time and energy to accomplish what you want out of life.	
12.	If people in your life are acting out of control, you are able to freely express your feelings of disappointment or disagreement.	
13.	If you feel intimidated by another person, you freely admit your feelings to yourself and choose not to let this person control the way you feel, think, or act.	
14.	You are able to admit feeling powerless over those things out of your control to change, fix, or rescue.	
15.	You are able to feel at ease and have serenity in letting go of the uncontrollable and unchangeable in your life.	
16.	You do not feel you are alone in having to deal with the pressures of life because you feel you have a Higher Power to whom you can handover the uncontrollable and unchangeable, over which you feel powerless.	
17.	You feel detached from the behaviours, actions, and negative aspects of the people in life for whom you care a great deal and yet are not able to fix, rescue, or change.	
18.	You are able to feel good about yourself with no guilt or remorse when you feel detached from the people with whom you have had toxic relationships in the past.	
19.	You do not let fantasies, dreams, traditions, or promises of the way things are supposed to be interfering with your rational experiences of life.	
20.	You have no need to be on guard against feeling hurt or pained, because you feel it is better for you to be vulnerable in life to experience authentic human growth.	

INTERPRETATION: If you checked 17 or less, then you need to work on control of your emotional life so that you cease to use over-control of other people in your life to feel good about yourself. You need to handle your own feelings and not give others the power to affect the way you feel or express your feelings. **Your feelings are something which you have the ability to control and change.** They, along with your thinking and actions, are the only controllable and changeable you can influence, alter, or change.

CONCEPT

10

Self-talk or Auto Suggestion

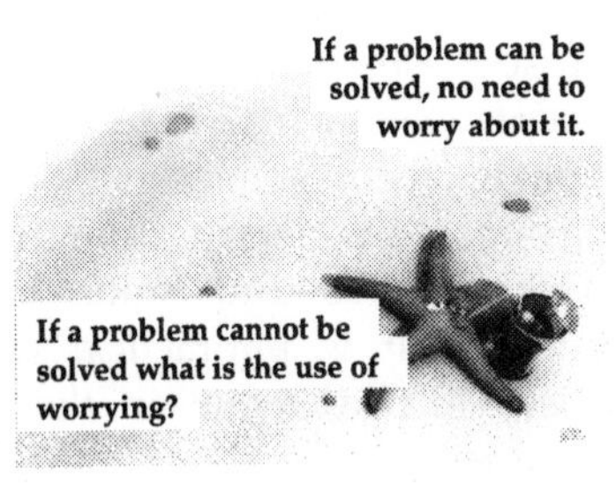

This technique is used to strengthen your 'internal locus of control'. Emile Coupe, a well known French Psychologist defines Auto Suggestion as ***'Implanting of an idea in oneself by oneself'***. According to him, whenever there is a friction between will and imagination, imagination invariably wins. When we use will power we tend to forcibly act in a certain manner without the backing of our sub-conscious mind. On the other hand, when we use our imagination, we strongly feed an idea into our sub-conscious, which is then translated into action, effortlessly.

Coupe goes on to explain that if a plank, one foot wide and 30 feet long is placed on the ground, people walk on it freely without fear of falling. If the same plank is placed between two towers, even the most daring person takes two steps and then comes back because **though his will is strong and pushes him forward, his imagination of falling**

prevents him from crossing the plank. But carpenters and high rise building workers cross such planks easily as they believe that it can be done. He explains that first of all we should know that auto-suggestion is possible and it can give rich dividends. Secondly, to know by what means it can be done. **Auto suggestion works on our sub-conscious mind.** Emily Coupe also says that

1. During auto suggestion, **'will'** should not come into play.
2. In the conflict between will and imagination, the 'force' of the imagination is in direct ratio to the square of the will.
3. When the will and imagination are in agreement, one does not add to the other, one is multiplied by the other.
4. Imagination can be directed.

Without our own knowledge we keep suggesting to ourselves from the time we can remember. We would not be aware of the effects of our own suggestions on ourselves. Now that we understand the concept, we can use it for our advantage. One has to continuously feed suggestions to improve health, memory, relationships, etc. **Every thought which fills our mind becomes true for us and tends to transform itself into action.** Therefore, it is impractical to suggest two things at a time, which contradict one another. This leads to a mental state of 'conflict'.

CONCEPT

11

The Second 'C' is Complain

The **'law of complementarity'** teaches us that there is nothing absolutely good and bad and they synergistically co-exist. Look back into your life dispassionately and observe how instinctively we all complain about everything that happens around us. We complain of heat in summer, rain in rainy season, cold in winter, traffic jams, noise, pollution, neighbors, colleagues, friends, wife, husband, children, parents, and the list goes on. Complaining is part of our life. If there is a paradigm shift in our minds, making us not to complain, we can focus our attention on better things in life. **If we stop complaining, we naturally become positive.** It is like saying the glass being half full instead of half empty. Let us see some incidents to know how the shift in our thinking can help us lead a happy life.

Enka and Manka are twin brothers. ***Enka is an incorrigible optimist who sees the bright side in every situation.*** Manka is highly pessimistic and finds fault with everything around him. Parents wanted to check if Enka could be made to complain in the worst circumstances and Manka could be made to feel happy with the best of things around him. They fill a room with horse dung and leave Enka in that room. They fill another room with the best of toys and leave Manka in that room. They tell both of them to play in that room for an hour. They go and open the room of Enka after an hour. They see Enka jumping happily on the horse dung. They ask Enka about his experience. He happily explains to them that every time he jumped on the horse dung, his feet were getting warmer because of the heat of the horse dung. Also he was happy doing so as the dung was very soft and exclaimed 'there has to be a pony around, as there is so much of horse dung!'

Then they go and open the room of Manka to find him sulking in a corner and crying. He starts complaining that he did not like the colour of one toy, the sound of another toy, the slow movement of the toy train, etc. He was so unhappy that he did not like even one toy among the whole lot! ***It is not the contexts which make us happy but it is our own state of mind, which makes all the difference.***

Another incident which is commonly talked about is that of two shoe salesmen visiting a desert to get some orders. One reports that he cannot do much business there, as nobody wears a shoe. The other reports that he sees a great opportunity there, as nobody wears a shoe and every body can be made to wear a shoe!

Two sisters are married to two brothers. The elder sister always complains about their mother-in-law to their parents. But the younger sister always talks good about the same mother-in-law. Parents decide to come and stay in their daughters' house and watch for themselves to know about the truth in their children's statement. They notice that whatever is told by the mother-in-law is viewed negatively and complained against by their elder daughter. Mother-in-law had lost her husband when her younger son was very small. She had taken great pains to educate her sons, who are now happily married and well settled today. Because the mother-in-law had gone through tough times in life, she was very particular about healthy living, discipline by keeping things in their respective places, using the available resources without wastage, etc. She was particular about early morning walks for health reasons, which was appreciated by her younger son and daughter-in-law. They preferred to join her for walks. But elder daughter-in-law felt that she is being unnecessarily harassed to get up early to walk as she dislikes getting up early. She has got the habit of keeping things wherever she sits and forgetting about it. Invariably every evening she goes out with her husband and eats out. Mother-in-law tells her to inform her in advance if they are not returning home for dinner as she can cook accordingly, which irritates the elder daughter-in-law. Parents assess the situation objectively and advise their elder daughter to step into the shoe of her mother-in-law and understand her concern, instead of complaining.

There are two things which can be learnt from the above examples. One is being pro-active and the other is being reactive. We are naturally reactive. Pro-active behaviour comes by training. One has to look at every situation by being pro-active and not by being reactive. Pro-activity gives wonderful results. Let us take an example.

There are three schools in the vicinity of a highway. Children have to cross the road to reach home. Many children die while crossing the road due to heavy traffic. People protest and blame the government for not taking action to prevent this. ***It is reactive behaviour.*** One gentleman who stitches covers for the two wheeler and four wheeler seats has a small shop on the side of the main road. He gets up from his seat, holds a long stick in his hand and stands guard stopping the vehicles to enable children to cross the road three times during the day. ***This is pro-activity.*** Which one do you think is successful?

CONCEPT

12

The Third 'C' is Compare

The 'law of Constructive Competition' teaches us instead of competing with others, we must compete with ourselves. We are aware that no two things are alike, yet we want every one to be alike or ideal. It is very natural for us to compare one another. We see parents comparing two children, teachers comparing two students, wife comparing her husband with some one else ...... Comparing never really helps. Each person is unique just as his/her thumb impression. **Problem arises in life when one is compared and continuously advised to change as per the ideal.** The husband compares his wife with his colleague and finds that his wife is quieter in her comparison and tries to change her to become like his colleague. Wife is happy the way she is and refuses to change. She tells her husband that he should learn to praise, but not try to perfect her.

Elder sister is married to a man who is the General Manager of a Company. Younger sister is married to a man who works between 10 am and 5 pm in an ordinary company and prefers to spend his free time with his wife and children. But the younger sister always compares her husband to her brother-in-law and is very unhappy that he is at home in the evening without looking for better options to come up in life. Parents visit her house once to find out the reason for her unhappiness. They tell her to stop comparing her husband with her brother-in-law. They ask her to look at the brighter side of things. They explain how the brother-in-law is working without rest which is causing stress leading to health problems besides differences with his wife for not being able to give time to the family. **Comparison does not create quality. Comparison and competition may bring out the darker side of a person instead of the brighter side.**

EXERCISE

Internal Development

We have elaborated how comparing does not help us to become success conscious. Now let us see as to how to strategize the process of our internal development through a line diagram.

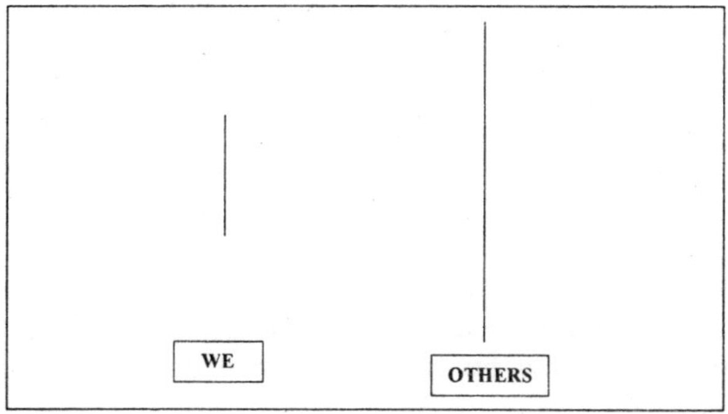

Look at the two lines shown above. We usually compare ourselves with others all the time and suffer from various complexes.

In the above line diagram, the small line is ours; the big line is that of a successful person called Unnathi. We compare ourselves continuously with her and feel that she is more good looking than us, wealthier than us, more popular than us, etc. and we are not able to tolerate this inferiority. So we start talking ill of her amongst the common friends. By doing so, we think that we are cutting her to size but people who hear us talk nonsense about Unnathi would be cutting us to size as they know what is Unnathi and wonder as to why we talk ill of her.

Instead of trying to cut some one to size by talking ill, we should pick up good things we notice about her and try to apply that in our life so that we are respected not only by others but also by ourselves. By doing so, we will be increasing the length of our growth line *vis-a-vis* that of Unnathi as shown below:

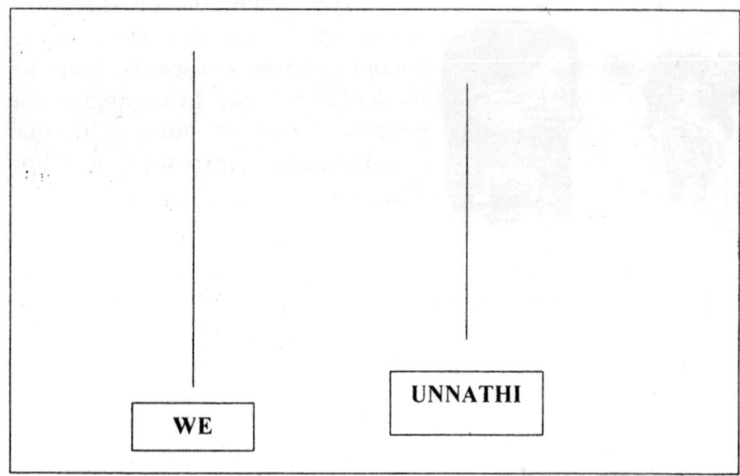

We need not grow by belittling others. We have to grow on our own merits. Please try to do this exercise vis a vis your ideal. Grow by competing each day with yourself not others.

CONCEPT

13

The Fourth 'C' is Change

The '**Law of inevitability of Change**' and 'Supremacy of Time', teaches us that change is bound to happen, yet it is rare for people to agree to change happily. If an employee is used to paper and files, he hates computerization. If a girl is used to wearing only modern clothes and after marriage, if she is asked to wear only a saree, she would find it suffocating. In the same way, if a girl is used to wearing only a saree and is forced to wear a low neck dress, she would find it extremely difficult to change. ***Many people feel proud to say that they will continue to be as they are and will not change.*** When we realise that change is inevitable, we have no other go. For example, we are adopting ourselves to Internet and computers today like never before. We cannot live without a mobile today.

We should not only be open to change but prepare ourselves for a paradigm shift also. Let us look at a few examples of a paradigm shift in our day-to-day life. We are traveling in a train. Each one in the compartment is busy in his/her, own way. One would be reading a book, other will be reading news paper, some one is listening to music, and some one is sleeping. In one of the stations, one gentleman with three of his children gets into the compartment, sits next to us and gets lost in his thoughts. His children start behaving in a very unruly manner, stamping on us, shouting, crying, and snatching away the book from us and so on. We get very annoyed about their behaviour and complain to their father, asking him to control them. Father says, 'Oh, yah, I am so sorry, children lost their mother an hour ago and they do not know how to take it. In fact, I do not know how to take it myself. I will control them. I am sorry'. There is a paradigm shift in the thinking of all the people in the compartment on hearing the story and every one tries to talk to the children and to sympathize with them. **If only we had tried to know about the truth in advance without any value judgment, a lot of unpleasantness could have been avoided.**

In another example, a newly married couple was sitting in a bus at the window seat whispering their sweet nothings. Opposite to them, a ten year old boy was sitting along with his parents and grand parents. That boy was talking animatedly about everything he sees outside. This irritates the newly wed couple. Suddenly it starts raining. The boy puts his hand outside and starts enjoying himself. The newly married man could not bear it anymore as rain was falling on him through the window opened by the boy. The man pulls the hands of the boy inside, shuts the window and shouts at the boy to behave and not to make noise continuously. Grandfather of the boy asks for his pardon and explains that the boy is seeing the world for the first time through his eyes, as he was blind by birth. They are returning after a major eye surgery of the boy that gave him vision which is making the boy playful and happy. **The man curses himself for being rude.**

In one more example, a boy comes back to live with his parents after 5 years of staying with his grand parents. He asks his father to come to his school the next day to attend parent-teachers meeting. Father asks the son to take his mother as he will not be able to take time off due to some urgent and important work. **The boy refuses to take his mother saying that she is very ugly and his friends would tease him about it.** Mother starts crying on hearing this. Father tells the son the following story.

'You were a small baby who was looked after by two full time servants. One day, accidentally your cradle caught fire. Both the servants ran away to save their lives leaving you behind. Your mother heard your screams from the kitchen. She came running and saved your life unmindful of what happened to her. In the process, you got some burns but your mother suffered severe burns on her face, hands and chest. You were treated and cured early whereas it took five years for your mother to undergo various surgeries to become normal. That is the reason you were staying with your grand parents. Now the treatment is complete and she feels that she can take care of you'. Boy cries on hearing this story. He goes to his mother, hugs her and says, 'You are the most beautiful mother on earth. I am very proud of you. I love you. You please come for the meeting with me tomorrow. I do not care what my friends say'. **Now, look at the picture below and tell us as you what you can see**.

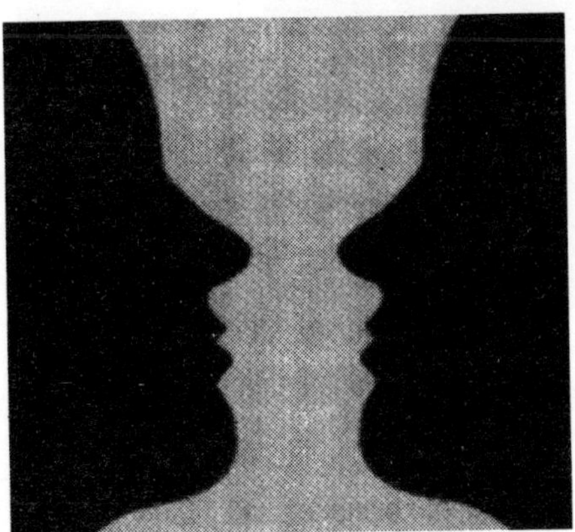

If you focus on the black, you will see two faces. If you focus on the white, you will see a vase. There are always two sides to a coin. We normally look at one side and make our own judgment. **Can we change at least after seeing the other side of the coin?**

CONCEPT 14

Changing Internally First

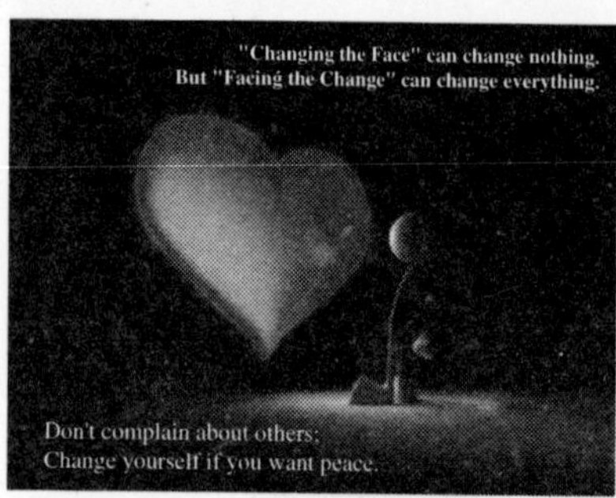

We commonly see everyone saying that there is a great need for changing our external world; we have to change the attitude of people. What we have to understand is that unless a person is changed internally by changing his limiting beliefs, no amount of external stimuli will help him change the poor image about himself. ***That is the reason it is said that it is better to teach a person how to fish than feed him a fish everyday.*** If an unemployed youth is convinced from inside that it is not good to live on subsidy but he should make an effort to get an employment, the youth tries his best to go out and find a job for himself.

Any change has to first come from inside. One should not have a **victim mentality.** Instead he should get into a **volunteer mentality**. One should learn to own responsibility than blaming every situation or everybody else for his present circumstances. Helping an individual in giving him sufficient self-confidence is more important than giving him some money at that point of time.

Feeding our sub-conscious mind with what exactly we want, such as good health, good money, good relationship will attract what we have aspired for, from the Universe. ***If one feeds only hatred, sickness, laziness, negative thoughts, he will receive only the mirror image of what he has fed himself.***

One has to sit in a calm and quiet place and think for sometime as to what exactly he wants. He has to note it down clearly and then start feeding that into his sub-conscious mind.

Let us start valuing ourselves

How do we see ourselves? Do we value ourselves? Do we feel internally confident of ourselves? If we give a word to someone, do we fulfil our promise? If we do, we feel confident of ourselves. We do what we say. This message goes to our sub-conscious mind. Whenever we happen to falter, our sub-conscious mind reminds us about our strength. If we don't correct our first mistake, our self-confidence is bound to suffer. To avoid such an event, we have to keep reminding ourselves about what we are and what we wish to do. For example: If we wish to leave cigarette or anger, our sub-conscious mind has to be firmly fed with these thoughts again and again.

Some people are very good at making promises. They are equally good at breaking them. As a result, their self-confidence breaks down and they meet failure again and again. It is said that, **if an egg is broken from outside force, life ends. If it breaks from within, a life begins. Great things always happen within.** Therefore, we need to strengthen our internal self rather than feeling bad about our external failures.

We must decide as to how we are valuable rather than how valuable we are. For example: there is no point lamenting about an incomplete house. If we spend our energies in completing the same, we can enjoy its comfort. No doubt there is no shortcut to hard work. It is not important how many times we fail but every time we fail we should try again with greater strength. **We don't drown by falling into water but only if we stay there and do nothing.**

The multifaceted potential lies within

Very often we are dependent upon others for our own decision-making. This makes us inactive. We lose sight of our own internal powers and tend to become victims of others' deceit. Then we spend rest of our lives regretting the same.

Driving our inner voice

Our sub-conscious keeps on telling our conscious mind that we are always right. If we feel helpless and depressed, our sub-conscious mind brings in all kinds of memories to reinforce the feeling. But if we consciously decide to be brave and positive, our sub-conscious mind will support our stance. **Our self-concept is not a product of single thought but emanates from series of thoughts, emotions and experiences.** Over the years, it keeps on consolidating itself. Others may give a good or bad opinion about us but unless we accept it, it does not affect self-concept. Therefore, we should be very careful while developing our internal beliefs. They should not be contradictory to each other. They should not be away from reality. We should keep testing our beliefs from time to time to guard against being misled in the long-run.

CONCEPT

15

The Fifth 'C' is Courage

'Law of Inter-connectivity' inspires us to work in harmony with others. Courage means being fearless. If we believe in oneness of humankind, fear of unknown will disappear. Many of us may not be born with courage. But we learn to be bold by reading about those who display courage at times of adversity or watching others or by associating with others and by training.

When Gandhiji said that independence can be fought by non-violence, nobody believed him. But he did not lose his courage of conviction and he proved himself right by sheer persistence.

Thomas Alva Edison did not lose his courage though he failed 99 times in his experiments with electric bulb till he succeeded in his 100th attempt.

Heller Keller did not lose courage though she was blind by birth. She became immortal with her work for the blind.

Committing suicide and ending one's own life on account of disappointment in love, job loss or financial losses, is shameful as it shows that one does not believe in oneself. **There is a solution for every problem.** Solution becomes visible when one thinks about the problem without losing courage. Getting into solution mode from problem mode always helps.

Many times our imaginary fears make us become weak and act like a mouse running for its life. If the situation is faced boldly, one feels confident like a tiger and the problem gets solved within no time.

One should show courage to condemn illegal, immoral and unethical acts but one should be scared while doing things which are illegal, immoral and unethical.

How to overcome fear?

Taking a small step at a time helps in getting rid of fear which enables us to take big steps subsequently. If we are scared of talking to strangers, we should learn to take the first step of smiling at strangers, at least to one person on a daily basis. Then we should try to talk to at least one stranger in a day, to get rid of our fears. This will help us to move ahead in freely talking and mingling with strangers.

Let us look at an incident. Uttam belongs to a middle class family where education is given great importance and generally everyone in the family believes that one should study well and get a good job. Uttam completes his engineering degree with good scores. His parents make all the arrangements for Uttam to go abroad for higher studies. **But Uttam is interested to pursue his interest in music for a living. Yet he is scared to express his feelings for the fear of his parents, peers, relatives and friends.** His lecturer understands his feelings and asks him to list out his fears. Uttam records his fears as follows:

1. Father will get into a fit of anger. He may shout. This may cause adverse effect on his delicate health
2. Mother may be disappointed. She feels proud and has been telling everyone that her son is going to

a foreign country to continue his studies and after getting employment, her son would invite her for a foreign tour

3. His sister and her husband will be disgusted. His sister had developed a feeling that he may find a suitable job for her and her husband also, in the foreign country.
4. His maternal uncles wish that he should be a role model for their children to study for engineering course. So entering into the field of music will be viewed poorly and they may start advising him against his foolish decision.
5. The children of his elder and younger uncles will treat him as inferior.
6. The children of his paternal mother-in-law have completed their higher studies and become famous in foreign countries. There will be a big discussion and all of them will engage in advising him.
7. His class mates will make fun of him as a mad fellow and they would look down upon him and not treat him as their friend.
8. He is not sure whether he would be successful in his chosen music field or not.
9. It may require more time for settling in life.
10. He may regret his decision in the future.
11. If he fails in his pursuit of music, he may find it difficult to come back to his engineering course.
12. The income that is obtained in the field of music may be much less than the income of an engineering graduate employee.

Time and again, Uttam was asked to list out the fears that come to his mind. He was asked to stop worrying and to explore his inner feelings to know whether his decision towards pursuing music was right by listing out the potential benefits. After being convinced about his decision, Uttam was asked to speak his mind to his parents. To his surprise, his parents understood his feelings and told him that they were interested in his welfare and whatever gives him happiness should be pursued by him. His relatives though tried to advise him, later understood his grit and determination and wished him luck. Uttam realized that if he had succumbed to his unfounded fears, he would have suffered all his life. Showing courage to face the situation can solve the problems easily.

Famous singer and music director Shankar Mahadevan pursued music after he became an engineer. Sanjeev Kapur became a celebrity chef by quitting engineering course in the middle, by pursuing his passion in food industry. ***It is better to ride on the courage than on fear to realize our dreams.*** If we learn to value these success conscious principles in life, there will be no place for fear.

EXERCISE

7

Analyze Your Fears

Please analyze your fears by putting 'X' mark for sentences applicable to you

S. No.	*Statement*	*X mark*
1.	I feel uncomfortable to talk to strangers	
2.	I do not like to get into arguments. I feel ashamed if I lose	
3.	I do not like to start anything new because I do not like to be insulted if I fail.	
4.	I don't speak out even if any one is doing anything wrong in front of me because I do not want to get into trouble later.	
5.	Under any circumstance I don't wish to be the first person to express my views or objections.	
6.	Unless I am forced, I do not like to disclose my views	

S. No.	Statement	X mark
7.	If some one expresses his opinion about my behaviour, even if it is true, I do not like to change.	
8.	I always prefer to continue with the traditional methods. If any body argues that these methods are unsuitable for the present times, then I get embarrassed.	
9.	When I like some one and they reject me, I get hurt	
10.	I feel very uncomfortable to discuss about my illness with doctors and hence I postpone going to doctor.	
11.	I always feel insecure about tomorrow.	
12.	If there is a mental setback to me, then I hesitate to express it to others. I am very much afraid about what other people think about me.	
13.	I tolerate other's behaviour despite being troubled by it.	
14.	I am not prepared to change my job though I am not happy in it for the fear that my family is dependent on me.	
15.	I do not like to take feedback, though it comes from my well wishers for my good. I avoid meeting such people.	
16.	I try to avoid inviting my friends and colleagues to my house as I am scared about their opinion about my house and my family members.	
17.	I prefer to be like everyone else. I would prefer to start something after some one else has started it.	
18.	I get bad dreams in my sleep very frequently.	
19.	I am always scared that the work that I do will be ruined.	
20.	I always feel that suicide is the only remedy if I commit any mistakes in my life.	

If your score for the above sentences is more than 3, then it means that you are suffering from fear of failure, fear of rejection, fear of unknown, etc.

CONCEPT

16

Creating a Shield Around Us

All our fears can be allayed if we have faith in the cosmic energy which is superior to all of us. A Hindu believer of God has various Gods with different virtues which are made use of in creating a shield around us. An illustration would explain this concept.

Swathi invites Ramya for her birthday party. Ramya is shocked when Swathi takes her to a pub. Ramya is from a traditional and conservative background and she does not like even a man going to pub, let alone a girl. She does not want even Swathi to go into the pub. What Ramya needs to do under such circumstances is to relax her mind completely and invoke Rama who is known for not doing anything wrong legally, ethically and morally. Within a few minutes Swathi either gets a call to return home or some distraction preventing her from taking Ramya to the pub for the party. Next time Swathi invites Ramya for the pub, Ramya can be on her guard.

Ketan is studying for the exams and is solving mathematical problems. He gets stuck with some problem and is unable to solve it. What he needs to do is to relax completely and invoke Ganesha, the problem-solver. Within minutes, solution strikes Ketan and he is able to solve his problem. In a similar fashion, we may make use of Hanuman for courage, Krishna for handling a situation diplomatically, etc. Christians make use of Angels to help them in times of need and Muslims call upon Prophet for help. This technique works wonders. One has to try it out to experience the results!

CONCEPT

17

The Sixth 'C' is Contribute

The **'law of seed'** or **'increasing returns'** shows that any act of goodness is rewarded by the Universe, many times over. When we are born, we are dependent. As we grow, we feel that we are independent and do not require anyone. But if we take a closer look at our life, we realize that we are inter-dependent for almost everything in life. We have been continuously receiving care from our parents, teachers, friends, school, college, relatives, strangers, etc. Let us see how and what we have been receiving so far.

Parents	They dream about our future even before we are born. They try to educate us in the best of schools; they sacrifice a lot to give us a good life. Sometimes they make property for us. They feel proud on our accomplishments. They bow their head in shame if we do something wrong but still pardon us and love us.
School/ teacher	Try to give us good education. They train us physically, mentally, socially, emotionally and teach us value of time, money and positive mental attitude. They feel proud to make us good citizens of the country.

Relatives/ Neighbours	They recognize our achievements and encourage us. If they find us doing something wrong, they don't hesitate to advise us.
Society	Good examples are obtained by looking into the lives of others in the society. It encourages us on our achievement and condemns and punishes us when we do wrong. We enjoy the freedom of speech and freedom to think from the society.
Nature	The elements of nature like earth, water, air, sun enriches our lives without any condition or expectation from us. It is always abundant and gives without any discrimination to every one It continues to give though we misuse it for our own selfish interests.

The list can be endless. Do we ever stop and think as to what we have contributed to our parents, our friends, our teachers and the nature? When we learn to give more than we receive, life turns out to be beautiful and meaningful. **A small change in our attitude of giving more than receiving leads us from success to significance.** Success is the value we give to ourselves whereas significance is the value we give to others. If we can make a list of what kind of contribution we can make to the society, it would enable us to think about what we are presently not doing. Let us take a few examples of how we can contribute to the society:

Parents	Taking care of parents who are old and not sending them to old age homes, Taking care of their medical expenses, To give them regular pocket money without asking for accounts, To take them to places which they would like to visit, To fulfil their desires without waiting for their request
Society	By not throwing plastic everywhere, the gutters would not get blocked and animals would be saved from suffering due to consumption of plastic, Not tuning the TV/radio with high volume which disturbs the neighbors,

Not talking loudly over mobile in public places,

Not spitting everywhere,

To give place to sit for children, women, old and handicapped people while traveling in a bus,

To help helpless people cross the road,

By not growing garden in front of the house by encroaching the roadside and troubling moving traffic,

By not throwing garbage of our house in front of the neighbor's house in order to keep our house and its surroundings clean,

By not letting our dog make a nuisance for others,

Not plucking flowers grown in the compound of some one else's house,

Donating blood for those in need,

Donating books to the library after having read a book,

Donating money to Orphanages or Old age homes, etc.

To donate in cash or kind to our Almamater or help our teacher in times of need,

Not to spoil the beauty of nature by our selfish acts like noise pollution, water pollution, air pollution, etc.

If we take a decision to contribute on a daily basis for 21 days and then observe the changes it has made in our lives, we notice that we would have become more and more refined in our life.

CONCEPT

18

Creating an Emotional Bank Account

Just like the deposit and withdrawal in a Bank, there is deposit and withdrawal in emotional bank account of life. ***Whatever good that we do is counted as deposit. Whatever we expect others to do is called as withdrawal.*** If the mother asks her son to go to a shop when he is studying and he agrees to take a break without complaining that he was disturbed when he was studying, is treated as a deposit. If the child completes his/her education without any problem, it is a deposit done by him/her with his parents. If the son supports the parents in times of need, it amounts to deposit. If the same son gets into financial trouble or mental stress due to some situation, his parents would reassure him that he need not worry and they are there to support him. That means to say that the son can withdraw when it is required if he has deposited earlier. If the son is a problematic son with the habits of lying, cheating and with bad habits and he gets into trouble at a later point of time, his parents would not bother about him as he has been only withdrawing and not depositing.

One can notice that people rush to participate in some functions of a relative or to extend help in times of need because that person has deposited all along by contributing in some way or the other to every one. Otherwise everyone makes an appearance only as a guest, comments and then goes off.

It is always beneficial to deposit by being pro-active and service minded than expecting everybody else to serve us.

CONCEPT

19

Life is a Mirror

Our present situation is a mirror reflection of our previous thoughts. Stand in front of the mirror and stretch your arms as if you are giving away something to some one. You will see the reflection of being given in the similar fashion. That means if you give something, you will receive manifolds from the universe. **The adage 'Give and you shall receive' works beautifully.** When we learn to give, universe will give back in some form or the other to us. Now stand in front of the mirror with an outstretched hand as if you are receiving something from some one. You will see a similar reflection of yours in the mirror. In other words, if you take something from some one which truly does not belong to you, universe knows how to take back hundred or more times from you in its own way.

We always crib about unforeseen expenses which are not under our control. Being caught at the traffic signal by a policeman for moving a few inches beyond the stop line and asked to pay a fine of Rs. 200 means that universe is taking it back from us in some form or the other. It is mainly because we have to pay back what does not belong to us. **Universe is a great teacher and knows how to hit and when to hit to teach a lesson to us.**

CONCEPT

20

The Seventh and Most Important 'C' is Choose

The law of cause and effect shows that what we get is a result of what we did. We have already learnt that thought forms help us to become what we want to be. There is nothing called a good day or a bad day. It all depends on your thoughts and actions. So, either you run the day or the day runs you. By choosing what we want through selection of the appropriate actions, would help us to grow. **'You become what you think about' is heard by us often and is one hundred percent true.'** If we observe the world carefully, we get to know that good and the bad co-exist. Similarly, health–sickness, prosperity–poverty, peace–restlessness, etc. co-exist. ***We have to learn to intelligently choose what we want.***

Santosh and Manish are brothers. Both of them share a room but have their own cot, table, cup-board, etc. to be comfortable. Both of them get the same training in values by their parents. Santosh chooses to be happy all the time where as Manish complains about everything all the time. Santosh's things are always orderly while Manish never finds his things when he needs them. Attitude of Santosh is not to procrastinate and do whatever he does with a sense of involvement, which makes him very popular. Manish, on the other hand does not feel like doing anything for others. So no one likes his company. Both have chosen a different way of life for themselves and are therefore squarely responsible for their consequences.

Bhavya has the reputation of being dependable, hardworking and one who has a positive attitude in the office where she works. When asked about her secret of success, she says, **'I come here to work. So I choose to work well with a positive mental attitude'.**

Ramya's mother-in-law was under treatment for some sickness. She gets lot of visitors to enquire about her health. She likes talking about her disease and enjoys the sympathies she gets from the visitors. In the process her condition becomes from bad to worse. One day her doctor warns her to stop talking about her sickness and encourages her to affirm that she is getting better day-by-day in every way to attract health and not sickness. **If we want to be successful in life, we should learn to attract health, happiness, prosperity, abundance, wealth, riches, peace and positive mental attitude.**

Remember the story of Alaudin and his wonderful lamp. Genie of our life will get us what we ask for! But the most important thing to remember here is that the Universe will never support if we wish bad for others as Universe always stands for everything that is fair.

If we look at the example of some successful people, every one thinks that this successful man has a 'Midas' touch! Whatever he touches becomes gold and so he is successful. But the fact is that the person would attract success irrespective of circumstances and he continues to become successful. Universe always supports those who believe in themselves and move ahead despite adverse circumstances.

'Law of Attraction' is working in the Universe all the time. Universe gives us whatever we ask for even upto one hundred times of our wish. So we should be very careful in choosing what we want. **We have to think hundred times before we do any work as we have no control over the consequence once the work is done.**

Lance Armstrong is a great example of choosing success in life. His life's mission was to become a professional cyclist and win 'Tour De France' competition which is tough. But at a very young age, he gets testicular cancer. He was advised by his doctors to give up cycling as he would be required to undergo chemotherapy and other medication. But he chooses to focus on his cure, getting back health, winning the cycling competition. **He survives cancer and wins 'Tour De France' competition not once but seven times.** His success is only because of his right choice. He did not choose moaning and cursing himself and his fate, for the situation he was in.

We may recall the story of a boy, Monty, which we read long ago. The teacher asks the students to write an essay on their 'dream' about what they would like to become when they grow up. Monty submits his essay to his teacher. Teacher returns the essay to Monty and tells him to re-write the essay as it is too optimistic. He warns that since it has to be evaluated for grades he should make it realistic and gives Monty two days time to submit. Monty goes home and asks his father about it. Father tells Monty that it is his dream and he should take a decision whether to re-write scaling it down or not. Monty submits the same essay to the teacher after thinking for two days and says to the teacher 'You can keep the marks as I choose to keep my dreams'.

After several years, Monty invites the teacher to his ranch for a party. The teacher attends the party along with his current students. **The teacher starts crying in the party and tells his students that he was a dream stealer all along.** He has snatched the dreams of his students and in the process responsible for making them ordinary. Only Monty had the courage to say that he would like to keep his dreams irrespective of the grade he receives and went on to achieve his dreams of owning a ranch of 600 acres with over 100 horses.

We may receive a lot of input from others but the final choice should be ours only, as we are responsible for our lives and in turn for many other lives that depend on us.

EXERCISE

Limitless Thinking

Having explained the success conscious principles, we have a small exercise for you. Take out a paper and a pen. Now write down what kind of a house you want to build, thinking that time and money is not a problem for you. After you finish, read out what you have written. Be honest in doing this exercise. It is our experience that people who are living in two bedroom house may increase the number of rooms to 3 or 4. Normally nobody writes about a house built in one acre or more with swimming pool, tennis court, lawn, garden, etc. It is mainly because we are always limited by our past or present experiences. **We have created a limitation within ourselves without our knowledge.** We cannot think beyond our present circumstances. We feel that dreaming is bad. We feel that we should be happy with what we have and not be greedy in expecting something beyond one's imagination. Remember the story of Alladin's Chirag?

We have to understand that there is no limitation to the nature or the universe. Nature is always abundant and provides for everyone. If we believe in God, we say that God is omnipresent, omnipotent and omniscient. But do we really believe that? If we believe that, there cannot be any limitation. **It is only lack of our understanding of our potential that creates these limitations.** Let us learn to think without any limitations. If we desire to achieve something big, it becomes a possibility if we believe in it without limitation as the thought that we leave to our sub-conscious mind and the universe will ensure to put us to work in the direction of achieving it. So let us practice thinking without limitation and observe how the thoughts become a reality. But we should remember one thing. ***Universe will never support us if we think negatively and to cause harm to others.***

CONCEPT

21

Success through Affirmations

We are aware of the fact that thoughts lead to action, action leads to habit, habit leads to character and character leads to our destiny or future. Strong thoughts have strong energy and weak thoughts have weak energy. There are 60,000 to 70,000 thoughts which pass through our mind on a daily basis. **Our sub-conscious mind will not be in a position to know which thought to work on.** So to make our thoughts strong, we have to affirm it on a daily basis. Affirmations are nothing but **auto suggestions** repeated more number of times to make the thoughts strong. We suggest writing the affirmations to enable our sub-conscious mind to take it into the deeper layers for manifestation. We suggest that the affirmations be written as many times as possible during the day to make it stronger.

When we do the affirmations, we use the present tense. We say affirmations as if we have already achieved whatever we intend to suggest. To give you an example, one boy had a dream of working at Microsoft. His affirmation was 'I am successfully employed at Microsoft office at Seatle,

USA and I am extremely happy'. He started affirming even before he completed his engineering degree. His affirmations pushed him into taking exams conducted by Microsoft Corporation and then getting into his dream job. Some examples of specific affirmations are as follows.

- It is Augut 2010 (specify time) and (write what you want to be).
- My monthly income is Rs. 40,000.
- It is June 2010, I am enjoying my holiday at Kullu valley with my family.
- I am happy and grateful that my weight is 50 kgs with my waist 26 inches with excellent health and energy.
- I am free from habit of smoking.

There should not be usage of any 'will' while affirming. It would be better to add words like 'I choose' which will trigger the imagination. An affirmation with an emotion attached to it like 'I choose to become slim with 50 kgs weight and 26 inches waist as it gives me happiness' works better.

We suggest that negative words like 'cannot', 'shall not', etc. should not be used while affirming. Instead of saying 'I do not suffer from headache', it is better to say 'I am free from headache'.

One of the famous affirmations of Emile Coupe, taught by him to his patients, which is being used the world over is 'Day by day, in every respect, I am getting better and better'.

Louis Hay in her book on healing suggests wonderful affirmations. Some of the famous and widely used examples of affirmations are given below.

- In the infinity of life where I am, all is perfect, whole and complete.
- I am an unlimited being receiving from an unlimited source in an unlimited way.
- Money is constantly circulating in my life. I release it with joy and it returns to me multiplied in a wonderful way. I use it for good only.

We encourage you to read the book on healing by Louis Hay for very good and **useful affirmations to heal most of the diseases.** The perfection of God is now being expressed through me. The idea of perfect health is filling my sub-conscious mind. The image God has of me is a perfect image and my sub-conscious mind recreates my body in perfect accordance with the perfect image held in the mind of God. My body and all its organs were created by the infinite intelligence of my sub-conscious mind. It knows how to heal me. Its wisdom fashioned all my organs, tissues, muscles and bones. This infinite healing present within me is now transforming every atom of my being, making me whole and perfect. I give thanks to the healing I know is taking place now. Wonderful are the works of creative intelligence within me.

- Day by day, in every respect, I am getting better, better and better.
- By day and by night, I am being prospered in all my interests.
- I am an unlimited being receiving energy from an unlimited source
- I am open and receptive to all the good and abundance in the universe.
- I am open and receptive to new avenues of income.
- I now receive my deposits of goodness from expected and unexpected sources.
- I am alive to the joys of living.
- I deserve and accept the very best in life.
- I love and approve of myself.
- I like money. I love it and I use it wisely, constructively and judiciously.
- I am grateful for the good and riches of my mind.
- I am one with the infinite intelligence of my sub-conscious mind. It is my right to be rich, happy and successful.
- I am forever conscious of my true worth. I give my talents freely and I am wonderfully blessed financially.

EXERCISE

Affirmations at the Beginning of the Day

Some of the time tested and well researched affirmations by various thinkers have been given below. Reading or writing them everyday has a tremendous impact. We request you to try them at least for a month.

AFFIRMATIONS AT THE BEGINING OF THE DAY

- My day begins with gratitude and joy.
- Today is a great day and I can do everything with the help of cosmos, which strengthens me.
- Today I begin a new life. I will greet this day with love in my heart.
- In the infinity of life where I am, all is perfect, whole and complete.
- I support myself and life supports me.
- I see evidence of the laws of Universe working all around me and in every area of my life.
- I reinforce what I learn in joyous ways.

- I look forward with enthusiasm to the adventures of the day, knowing that in my life, all is good.
- I am living, loving, joyous expression of life. All is well in my world.

NIGHT AFFIRMATIONS

- I thank that I am rich in my mind and my affairs.
- As I sleep, my creative mind will work out ways and means of guiding me in thought and action, so that when awake, I think the thoughts and do the things that will enable me to manifest mental and material riches.
- Every night from the time I wish to go to sleep till the time I wish to wake next morning, I sleep deeply, calmly and quietly and in waking I feel perfectly well, cheerful and active.
- All my organs are performing their function properly. My heart beats in a normal way and the circulation of the blood takes place as it should. The lungs are carrying out their functions, as also the stomach, the intestines, the liver, the spleen, the kidneys and the bladder. My brain is functioning properly with alertness, intelligence, wisdom and vitality. My nervous system, my circulatory system, my digestive system, my muscular system, my excretory system, every cell in my body is functioning perfectly well and properly.
- I thank the Cosmos.

CONCEPT

22

Using the Mirror to Strengthen Affirmations

Try to make a person who is crying, to stand in front of the mirror and cry. They cannot do it because they do not want to see themselves unhappy.

Using the mirror to improve one's posture and confidence is a well tried technique. Best speakers are born by using this technique to fight stage fear. In fact, the entire speech is practiced by some in front of the mirror to get the best possible effect on the audience.

To give an example, if a young man has failed in a few interviews, his confidence would be low to face the next interview which would be scheduled in the coming few days. In such a situation, the young man should **stand in front of the mirror, look into his own eyes in the reflection and address himself loudly**. He should say 'forget about the past interviews. You are sure do extremely well in the interview which is coming upon ... date. You are a winner and you will always be a winner'. This technique can be applied while taking a shower or when you are on a hill top or some vast place with privacy.

The above exercise brings a person face to face with his/her inner self. He/she communicates with the sub-conscious mind and feeds what is desired through affirmation. The stronger the affirmations, stronger is the thought form and consequent outcomes.

CONCEPT

23

Visualization

It is noticed that sub-conscious mind identifies itself with pictures very fast. **Visualization technique is seeing affirmations as pictures in our mind.** It improves the self confidence in achieving our goals to a great extent.

Olympic athletes and successful people use this technique very extensively. To give an example, the boy who dreamt of working in Microsoft office should see himself walking into the huge office of Microsoft, sitting and working on computer, participating in meetings, etc. repeatedly.

If the affirmation and visualization are done without having a feeling that you are the person in the picture and the writings, the sub-conscious mind also feels that it is not for you but for some body else. **So it is important to put emotions into our affirmations and visualization techniques.**

The first step for anything is the thought. The thought leads to action of setting a goal and doing what is necessary for achieving the goal.

Goals are not just promises, they are commitments.

Goals are not just wishes, they are visions.

Goals are for the serious minded people who intend to become significant in life.

Future is not what we see tomorrow. Every second spent with vision now, is the future in our hands. Today's actions are the resultant future tomorrow.

CONCEPT

24

Whether Seeing is Believing?

As each bird flaps its wings, it creates uplift for the bird following.

In a V formation, the whole flock adds at least 71% more flying range than if each bird flew alone.

Normally we all feel that we cannot believe anything till we see it happen. We tend to believe what we see. We see what our eyes show us. This sight is interpreted by each one of us in the context of our past experiences, our beliefs and environmental factors. Hence same sight is viewed differently by different people. **If our beliefs are unfounded, we are bound to see things in a wrong perspective. Ordinary people first see and then believe, but all** successful people first believe in themselves and then see it happening as they believe. **So the success MANTRA is "believing is seeing" and not "seeing is believing".**

In visualization techniques, we suggest that 'Believing is seeing'. One should first believe that they have got whatever they want by seeing themselves in the mind's picture first and it becomes a reality later on. Suppose we want to buy a particular car. We happen to notice only that car on the roads. We tend to hear more and more things about the same car. Hence, we attract what we want to in terms of what we hear and what we see. Only precondition is that we should be focused on what we want.

Most often our minds are full of worries and problems. **As soon as we wakeup, we think about what we have not been able to achieve. We start planning as to how to achieve them and how to solve our problems. That means, all the time our mind is occupied either by problems or worrying about their solutions. Are we not compromising with our quality of life by such behaviour? We need to keep pace with our life and not encounter it negatively.** Hence, Unburden exercise and fish Bone Analysis would help us deal constructively with our problems.

We should be very clear as to what we want in life. **Only then we can be clear as to how to achieve our goals. Our mind usually keeps wandering with thousands of thoughts. But with clarity of goals, we are able to eliminate all the useless thoughts and ideas and focus only on the cherished goals. For example, as a student our goal is to achieve 90% marks in the exam. If we believe and visualize that we are able to remember everything that we read, understand our subjects and have a tremendous memory power, our sub-conscious mind accepts this as true. We may not have been successful earlier but now there are no doubts in our mind about our future success. Our self-image has changed from failure to success. However, we must give our 100% to this goal of ours and not distract ourselves with anything else.**

Nobody can stop an idea whose time has come. **Once an idea fixes itself strongly in our mind and our thought process starts in that direction, nothing can stop it from materializing. Most scientists come up with their discoveries and inventions in this manner. We get what we choose.**

The universal truth is that whatever we choose that in turn chooses us. **It is natural for every human being to have certain beliefs. Our beliefs in achieving success lead us to success. For example, we are not happy with the present** state of affairs of our job. We wish to change our job thinking that a new job may give us more satisfaction. Similarly, we may not be happy in our married life.. We may think that by divorcing our spouse, we may get a better companion and lead a happier life. Usually our beliefs are as follows:

- My present situation is not good enough, it could be better.
- More and more money and facilities are desirable, it is never enough.
- I will be happy only when I get all that I want.

However, it may so happen that after carrying out the above changes, we may lose whatever happiness we had earlier. Thus the truth is that happiness comes from within and not from external world. If we see the faces of great people we may notice the ever lasting happiness, composure and satisfaction, which is self-driven. They are always happy because happiness comes from within us. Therefore, whatever we do, we should do with great satisfaction without 'complaining and comparing'. Whatever we get, we go on accepting it happily. We plan with conviction, for what we wish to achieve in our future, achieve it and enjoy it with satisfaction. We never harbor the feelings of having been deprived of anything. If we did not have our eyes, we would be still happy that we have all other parts of the body in good condition. We would make efforts to see if we can get back eye sight and if possible we make it our goal and achieve it. If we realize that there are no such possibilities, then we decide to lead a good quality of life without the eyes. We do not get struck with the problem of not having the eyes. Instead we make use of other body parts, efficiently and effectively. As we become clear in our mind about our goals, the world also responds to us with equal clarity. Our sub-conscious mind prepares us to act in such a manner that leads us to our goals.

Our beliefs give rise to our mindsets. Most often we find that our success or failure is determined by our mindsets. Mindsets are neither constructive nor destructive. They are neutral. They work according to our goals. If we want to become a successful politician, we cannot afford to be an introvert. If we have an inward looking mindset, we cannot mix up with others and work in public field. If we have to achieve our goal then we must start visualizing that we are meeting large number of people, understanding their problems and working together with others for public welfare.

Our mindsets are based on our past bringing up and present situation. **Our sub-conscious mind accepts this picture of ours and defends it against any attempts to change. It revolts whenever we challenge our existing mindsets in the face of new situations. Our sub-conscious mind tells us that what we have been used to doing and thinking is right and therefore there is no need to change. In order to convince our sub-conscious mind we have to establish our changed picture through repeated visualizations. These visuals cannot be compared to viewing a cinema because we attach emotion with each aspect of change.** Thus changes of mindsets can happen only through a combination of affirmation and visualization.

We all create artificial boundaries for our self based on our past experiences and environment. **We do not imagine the vast world beyond these boundaries. We are very selective in hearing, seeing or believing in what we want to hear, see or believe. This is like putting blinkers on the horses. We act in a predetermined fashion; failing to appreciate that there can be different solutions to our problems. This creates a prejudice in our thoughts and behaviour. The biggest victim is our own potential which we are unable to imagine and utilize. For example, we need some money to purchase something of our choice.** Our energy is spent on how to save money from existing expenses rather than how to earn extra money for making this purchase. **Earning extra money requires us to go beyond our existing boundaries and try something new. Unless we are confident to try this successfully, we will not have the courage to change.**

Changing forcibly is bound to fail. **If we keep telling**

our self "I have to get up early in the morning", "I have to work hard for my exams", etc., our sub-conscious mind refuses to accept it. In fact, it makes us do exactly the opposite of our resolve e.g. if we put the alarm for getting up at 5.00 o'clock in the morning with firm determination, we actually end up pressing the alarm in the morning, resolving to get up after another 5 minutes. Finally, we get up at 7.00 o'clock, which is even later than our usual time to get up. On the contrary, if we make an affirmation that "I choose to get up at 5.00 o'clock in the morning to achieve my goals", our sub-conscious mind happily accepts it as a part of our self and helps us in getting up exactly at 5.00 am.

Only by replacing "I have to" with "I choose to", we can ensure our success. For example, we wish to get a gold medal in our exam. However, we obtained only 50% marks in our last exam. The natural response to our wish would be that it is impossible for us to get a gold medal. Others will also feel the same way. But if we are convinced that nothing is impossible for us, then we have to change our picture in our own mind. We should be able to visualize that we have got the gold medal, we are using our capabilities to the maximum and we are enjoying our success. Our sub-conscious mind readily accepts this visualization with emotions of happiness and inspires us to work very hard till we achieve the gold medal.

Under many situations, not taking a decision is also a decision. When we do not learn as to how to take decisions ourselves and allow others to decide for us, our sub-conscious propagates the same tendency all our life. Therefore, we should encourage young children to take their own decisions, right from childhood.

Some decisions may be right, some may be wrong. Yet every decision helps us to take a better decision next time. Once, a journalist asked a successful businessman in an interview, "How is it that all your ventures are always successful?" The business man answered, "Due to my experience." "How did you get this experience?" Journalist asked. "Because of taking wrong decisions", answered the businessman.

We do not take decisions because we are scared of failure. **If the others give us some advice and we do not follow it, then we are scared that they will feel bad about us and our relationships will get spoilt. Either way, unless we learn to take our own decisions boldly, we cannot achieve success. Our decisions have to be decided by our choices for our life goals. The goals are not just assurances, they are binding. Goals are far sighted.** Dreams do not come looking for us. We have to look for own dreams. **Goals do not come out of our intellect but they arise straight from the heart. Once we realize the benefits that we will experience by achieving the goal, it becomes easier for us to achieve them. According to psychologists each one of us works for two reasons. Either it gives us pleasure or it prevents any harm to us. Our daily 'Affirmations' would help us in overcoming our fears and attracting strong thought forms to realize our dreams.**

It is said that if the path is beautiful, please check the destination it leads to. But if the destination is good, never mind how difficult the path is. **Once we decide our goals we must write them down. The bigger goal should be sub-divided into smaller mile stones, which should be evaluated every now and then. This makes our thoughts very clear. We can then fix the specific actions required to achieve the goal. Our time and energy does not get wasted by distractions. We must analyze our present situation, and write down the difficulties which we are likely to face in the process of goal achievement. If we believe that the obstructions will not let us achieve our goal, we must write the benefits that will accrue to us, by overcoming these obstructions. If we visualize our goal in a motion picture form, experiencing the pleasures of achievement, confusion in our mind will disappear.**

Affirmation and visualization will thus help us use our sub-conscious mind to reach our goals. **We should be taking the following precautions:**

- Avoiding use of any negative words e.g. I should not get angry.
- We should fully focus on our goals.

- Goal should be realistic and focused rather than multi-faceted.
- We should keep our goals, affirmations and visualizations as our secrets. They should be disclosed only after achieving them.
- We should be specific in our goals which can be broken into smaller goals, e.g. If we wish to lose weight we should fix a time frame and within that fix smaller targets for losing weight.
- We should never have any negative goal for any other person as law of universe does not support that.
- Let us say that we "choose" to rather than 'wish' or want to.
- Repeatedly let us write our goals on paper at least 15 times or more a day, to make the thought strong enough.
- The goals can not be based on comparisons with others rather they should be comparing oneself in present state *vis-a-vis* the chosen state.
- The affirmation can not be with respect to changing other persons. It works on one self alone.
- The change in others can be brought only after changing oneself.
- We do not have any control over others.
- Let us attach emotions to the chosen goal.
  Let us 'visualize' that we have achieved the goal and feel all the emotions connected with that achievement.
- Our beliefs and visualizations should match each other.
- We must take responsibility for ourself and not try to depend on others or blame others.
- There is no place for any self doubt.

The universe has enough to give each one of us. Then why should we create chaos, confusion and conflicts by competing with each other and refusing to realize our own inner potential? We have to use its eternal laws of "attraction" **to get what we want. All we need to do is to**

spend a little more time towards the mental activities and we would be saving a life time full of fears, struggles, frustration and deterioration. We have to ensure that our conscious, sub-conscious and super-conscious mind work in tandem, to create a desired future.

Instead of trying to control others, let us take charge of ourselves. Instead of complaining about things that lie beyond us, let us be pro-active in removing the unpleasantness around us. Instead of comparing ourselves with others, let us invest in growing on our own merits. Instead of resisting positive change, let us work towards the paradigm shift by changing internally. Instead of being bogged down by fear of the unknown, let us show the courage to realize our dreams by valuing our self. Instead of always being in the receiving mode, let us learn to contribute to the society which brings manifold returns to our emotional bank account. Finally, instead of waiting for the lady luck to choose us, let us make a clear choice in favour of achieving success. By using the above techniques of unburdening, opposite thinking, goal setting, fish bone analysis, auto-suggestion, limitless thinking, affirmation and visualization, we can choose to create our own future and contribute to a healthy and prosperous society.

With our future is in our own hands, let us enjoy a bright and prosperous future!

References

1. You can heal your life by Louise L. Hay
2. Power of your sub-conscious mind by Dr. Joseph Murphy.
3. Self-mastery through conscious auto-suggestion by Emile Coupe.
4. God's Debris—A thought experiment by Scot Adams.
5. Zero resistance living by Dr. Maxwell Maltz (CD).
6. What you say when you talk to yourself by Shad Helmstetter.
7. Psycho Cybernetics by Dr. Maxwell Maltz.
8. Suggestion & auto-suggestion by Charles Baudoin.
9. The Secret by Rhonda Byrne.
10. Power of positive thinking by Norman Vincent Peale.
11. Beyond positive thinking by Dr. Robert Anthony.
12. Think and grow rich by Napolean Hill.
13. The success system that never fails by Clement Stone.
14. Seven habits of highly effective people by Stephen Covey.
15. Strangest secret by Earl Nightingale (CD).
16. Unlimited Power by Anthony Robins.
17. Principle Centred leadership by Stephen Covey.
18. Magic of thinking big by David Schwartz.
19. Say yes to your potential by Skip Ross.
20. Dynamic living seminar by Skip Ross (CD).
21. While You Are Stuck In A Traffic Jam, I'm Playing Golf by Simon Thompson.
22. Tough Times Never Last, but tough people do! by Robert H. Schuller.
23. Nine Steps to successful living by Mohinder Singh Walia.

Index